FIRST 50 BLUES SONGS

YOU SHOULD PLAY ON GUITAR

ISBN 978-1-4950-9561-0

HAL•LEONARD®

Visit Hal Leonard Online at
www.halleonard.com

Contact Us:
Hal Leonard
7777 West Bluemound Road
Milwaukee, WI 53213
Email: info@halleonard.com

In Europe contact:
Hal Leonard Europe Limited
42 Wigmore Street
Marylebone, London, W1U 2RN
Email: info@halleonardeurope.com

In Australia contact:
Hal Leonard Australia Pty. Ltd.
4 Lentara Court
Cheltenham, Victoria, 3192 Australia
Email: info@halleonard.com.au

CONTENTS

All Your Love
(All of Your Love)

Words and Music by Samuel Maghett

Key of B

Intro
Moderately slow

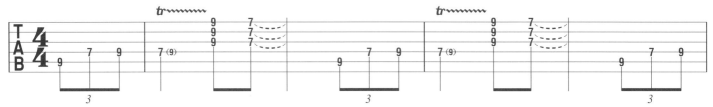

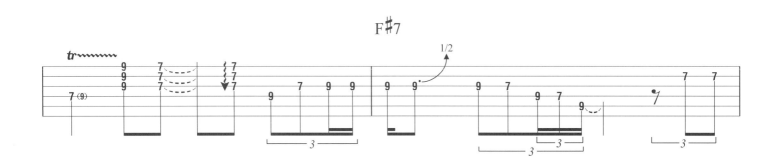

1. All

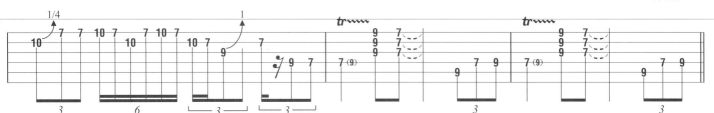

Verse

B7		E7			B7

etc.

of your love,   ba - by,   can it be mine?

2., 4. *See additional lyrics*
3. *Instrumental*

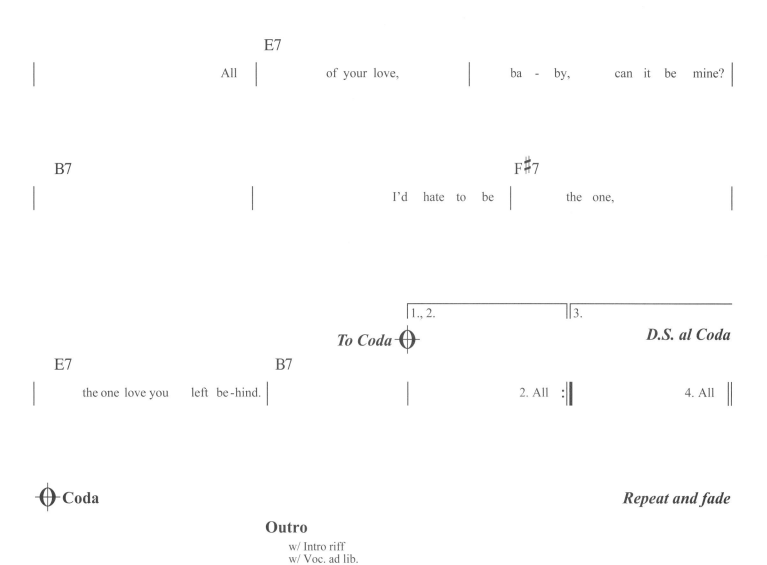

E7

All | of your love, | ba - by, can it be mine? |

B7　　　　　　　　　　　　　　　　　　　　　**F♯7**

| | I'd hate to be | the one, |

| 1., 2. | 3. |

To Coda ⊕　　　　　　　　　　　　　　　*D.S. al Coda*

E7　　　　　　　**B7**

| the one love you left be-hind. | | 2. All :‖ 4. All ‖

⊕ **Coda**　　　　　　　　　　　　　　　　　　*Repeat and fade*

Outro
w/ Intro riff
w/ Voc. ad lib.
B7

| ‖: | :‖

Additional Lyrics

2. All of your love, baby, don't throw it around.
   All of your love, baby, don't throw it around.
   Love is one thing, baby,
   You won't find on the ground.

4. All of your love I've got to have one day.
   All of your love I've got to have one day.
   Don't you leave me, baby,
   Baby, please come back this way.

All Your Love
(I Miss Loving)

Words and Music by Otis Rush

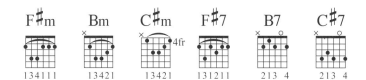

Key of F♯m

Intro

Moderate Rhumba

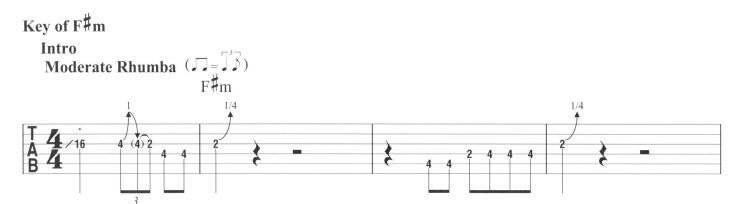

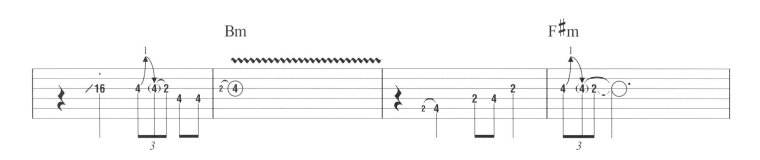

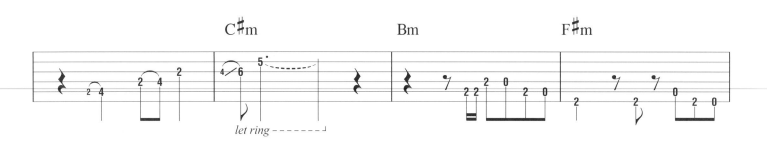

𝄋 Verse

N.C.   F♯m

1. All the love I miss   lov-in',   all the kiss I miss   kiss-in'.

2. *See additional lyrics*

3. *Instrumental*

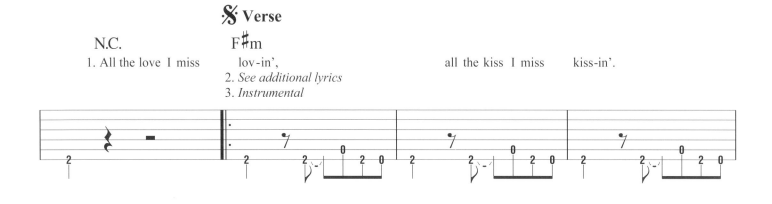

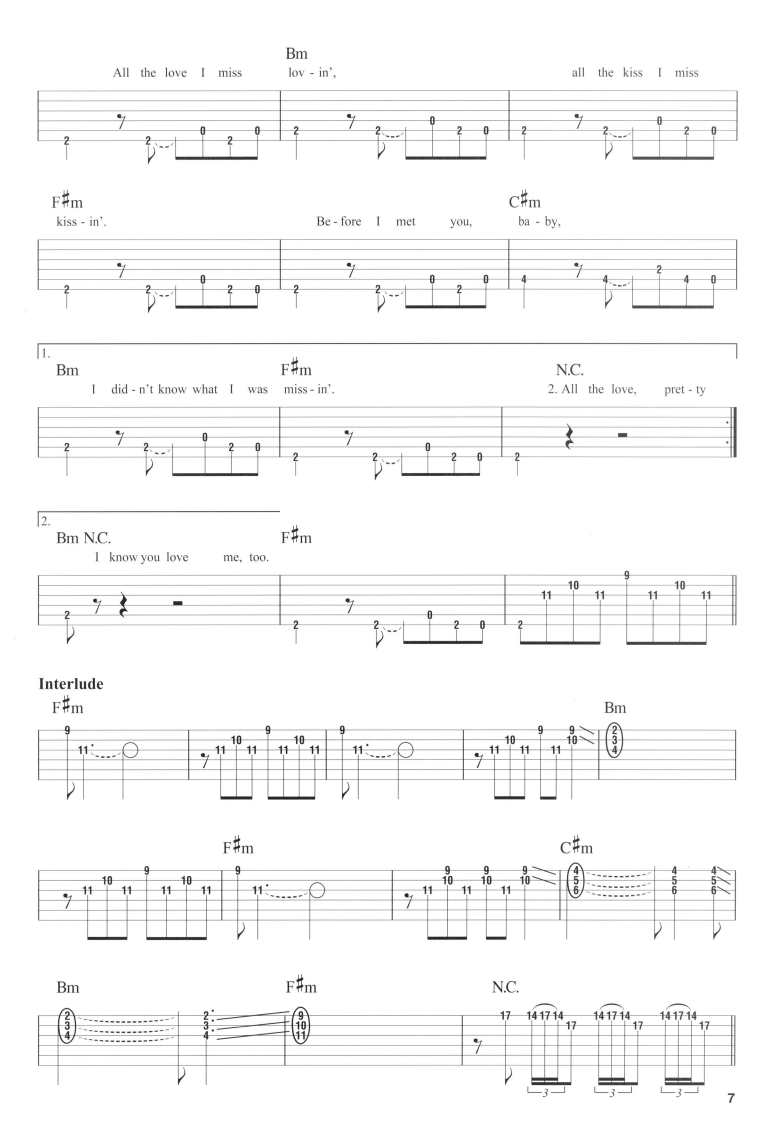

Key of F#
Guitar Solo
Swing feel

F#7

B7   F#7

C#7   B7   F#7

Whoa,

Chorus

F#7

| whoa, whoa, ba-by. | | You know I | love you, ba - by. | | Yeah, |

B7   F#7

| yeah, ba-by. | | You know I | love you, ba - by. | | I |

D.S. and fade

C#7   B7   F#7

| love you, ba - by. | | Oh, I love you | so. | | ‖

Additional Lyrics

2. All the love, pretty baby, I have in store for you.
All the love, pretty baby, I have in store for you.
The way I love you, baby, I know you love me, too.

Hide Away

By Freddie King and Sonny Thompson

Key of E

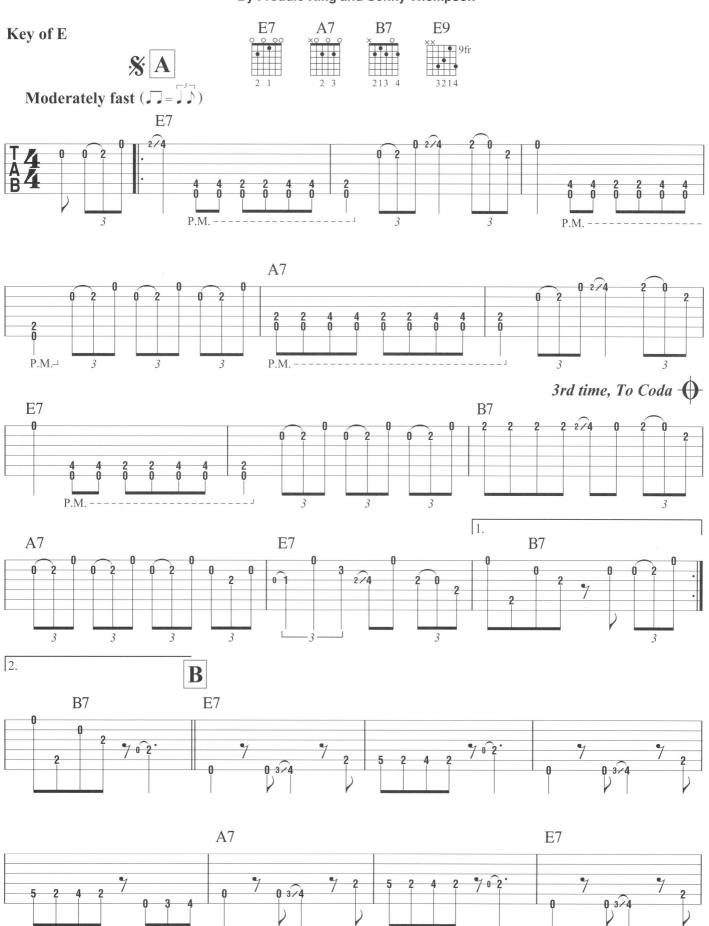

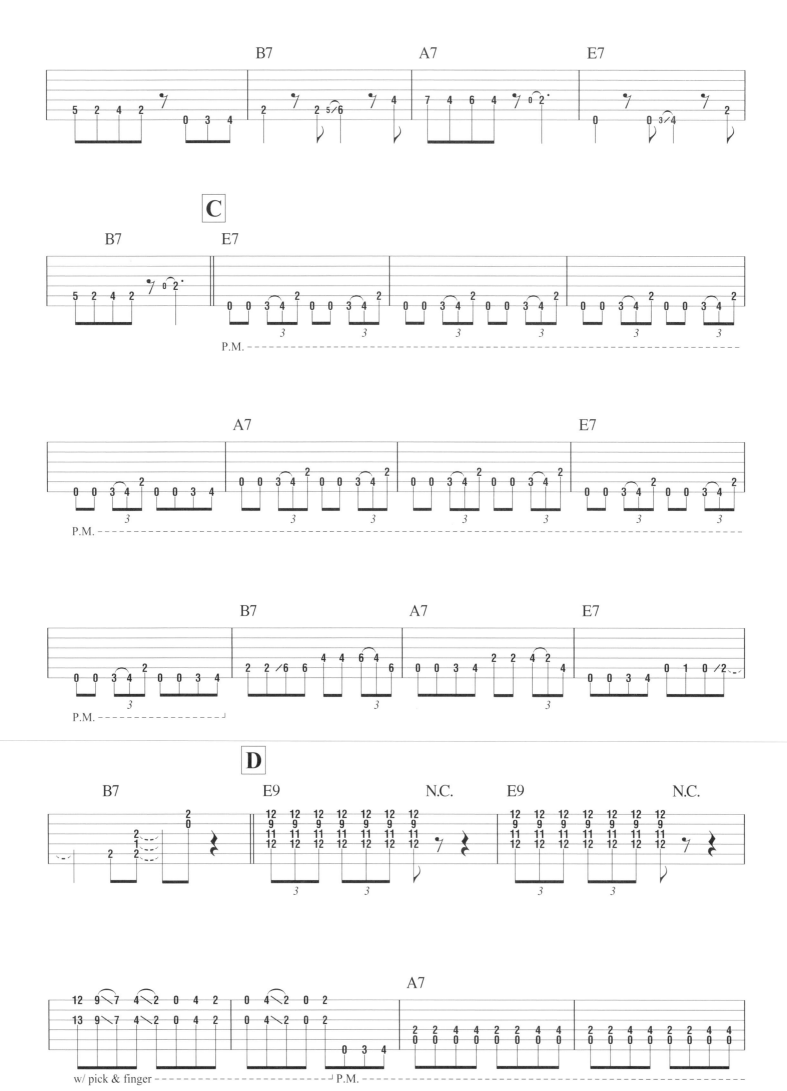

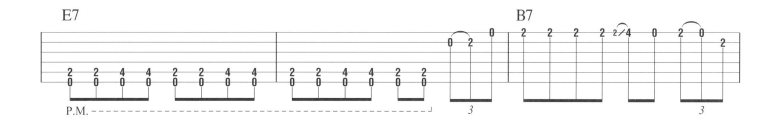

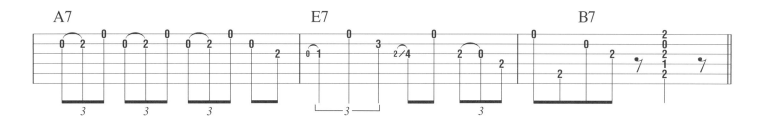

E (♪♪ = ♪♪)

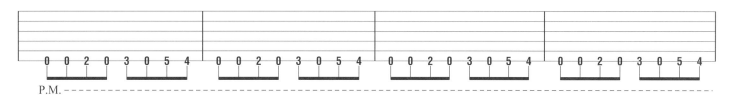

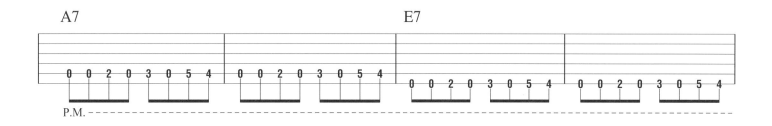

D.S. al Coda

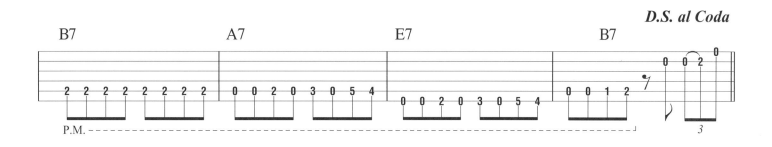

⊕ Coda

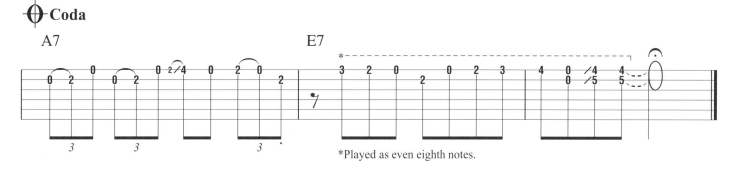

*Played as even eighth notes.

11

Baby Please Don't Go

Words and Music by Joseph Lee Williams

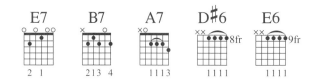

Capo III

Key of E
Intro
Moderately fast

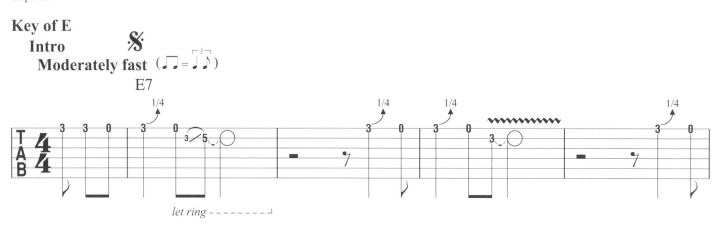

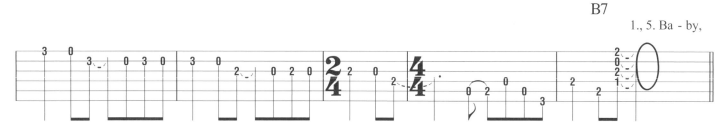

1., 5. Ba - by,

Verse

E7

‖: please don't go, | | ba - by, | please don't go, | | ba - by, | please don't go { down to / back to }

2., 3. *See additional lyrics*

|1., 2. | |3.
B7 | B7

New Or-leans, you know I | love you so.
New Or-leans and get your | cold ice cream. } | 2. Be-fore I :‖

Solo

E7

A7   E7

B7 A7 E7 A7 E7 B7

4. You brought me
6. *See additional lyrics*

Verse

E7

| way down here, | | you brought me | way down here, | | you brought me |

To Coda

D.S. al Coda (take 3rd ending)

E7 A7 E7 B7

way down here by the roll - in' fog, you treats me like a dog.

Coda

Outro-Verse

E7 B7 E7

You know your | man done gone, | you know your |

man done gone, | you know your | man done gone down the |

E7 A7 E7 D♯6 E6

coun - ty farm; he's got his shack - les on.

Additional Lyrics

2., 6. Before I be your dog,
Before I be your dog,
Before I be your dog,
I get you way'd out here
And let you walk alone.

3. Turn your lamp down low,
Turn your lamp down low,
Turn your lamp down low
And I'll beg you all night long,
Baby, please don't go.

Baby, What You Want Me to Do

Words and Music by Jimmy Reed

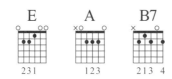

Key of E

Intro

Moderately

E

1. You got me

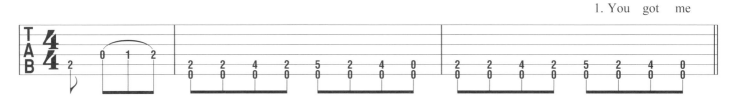

℅ Verse

E

etc.

‖: run - nin',   you got me | hid - in',   you got me | run, hide, hide, run an -|

2., 3. See additional lyrics

                                 A   E

| - y - way you wan - na let it | roll.   Yeah,   yeah,   yeah. |

                              B7   A

| You got me | do - in' what you want me, | ba - by, why you wan - na let go? |

| 1. | 2. |

E   B7   B7

                                       2. Go - in'

Interlude

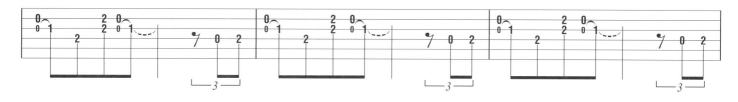

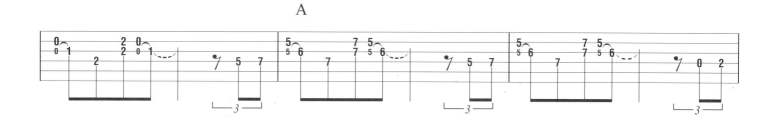

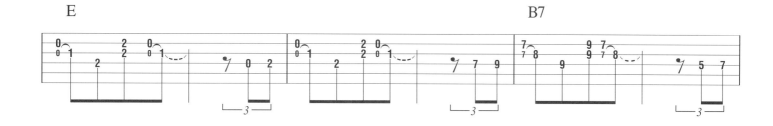

D.S.
(take 2nd ending and fade)

3. You got me

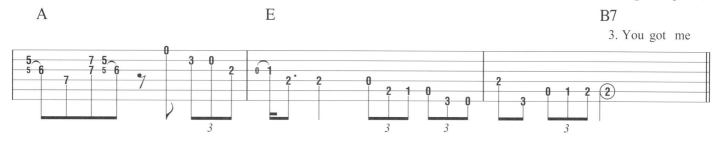

Additional Lyrics

2. Goin' up, goin' down,
   Goin' up, down, down, up anyway you wanna let it roll.
   Yeah, yeah, yeah.
   You got me doin' what you want me, baby, why you wanna let go?

3. You got me peepin', you got me hidin',
   You got me peep, hide, hide, peep anyway you wanna let it roll.
   Yeah, yeah, yeah.
   You got me doin' what you want me, baby, why you wanna let go?

Bad to the Bone

Words and Music by George Thorogood

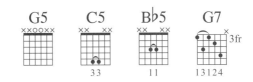

G5   C5   Bb5   G7

Key of G
Intro
Moderately

G5   C5 G5 Bb5   G5   C5 G5 Bb5

Play 7 times

Verse
G5   C5 G5 Bb5 G5   C5 G5 Bb5

1. Now, on the day   I   was born,   the nurs-es all   gath-ered 'round,
2., 4., 6. *See additional lyrics*
3., 5., 7. *Instrumental*

G5   C5 G5 Bb5 G5   C5 G5 Bb5

etc.

and they gazed   in wide won-der   at the joy   they had found.

G5   C5 G5 Bb5 G5   C5 G5 Bb5

The head nurse   spoke up,   said, "Leave   this one a-lone."

G5   C5 G5 Bb5 G5   C5 G5 Bb5

She could tell   right a-way   that I   was bad   to the bone.

Chorus
G5   C5 G5 Bb5 G5   C5 G5 Bb5

Bad   to the bone.   Bad   to the bone.

G5 · · · · · · · · · C5 G5 B♭5 · G5 · · · · · · · · · · · · · C5 G5 B♭5

B, b, b, b, b, b, b, bad. · · · · · · · · · · · B, b, b, b, b, b, b, bad.

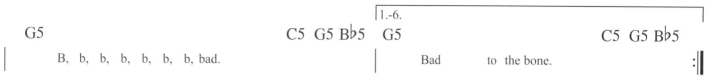

G5 · · · · · · · · · · · · · · C5 G5 B♭5 · G5 · · · · · · · · · · · · C5 G5 B♭5

1.-6.

B, b, b, b, b, b, b, bad. · · · · · · · · · · · · Bad · · · · · to the bone.

7.

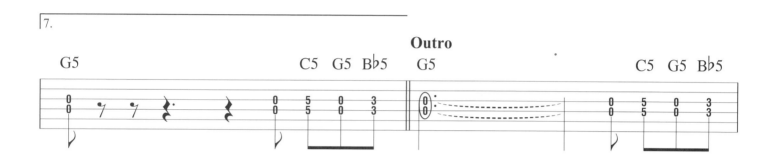

Outro

G5 · · · · · · · · · · · · · C5 G5 B♭5 · G5 · · · · · · · · · · · · C5 G5 B♭5

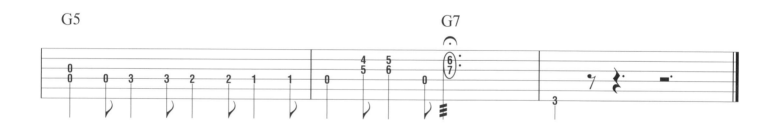

G5 · G7

Additional Lyrics

2. I broke a thousand hearts before I met you.
   I'll break a thousand more, baby, before I am through.
   I wanna be yours, pretty baby, yours and yours alone.
   I'm here to tell you, honey, that I'm bad to the bone.

4. I'll make a rich woman beg, and I'll make a good woman steal.
   I'll make an old woman blush, and I'll make a young girl squeal.
   I wanna be yours, pretty baby, yours alone.
   I'm here to tell you, honey, that I'm bad to the bone.

6. Now, when I walk the streets, kings and queens step aside.
   Every woman I meet, heh, heh, they all stay satisfied.
   I wanna tell you, pretty baby, what I see I make my own.
   And I'm here to tell you, honey, that I'm bad to the bone.

Before You Accuse Me
(Take a Look at Yourself)

Words and Music by Ellas McDaniels

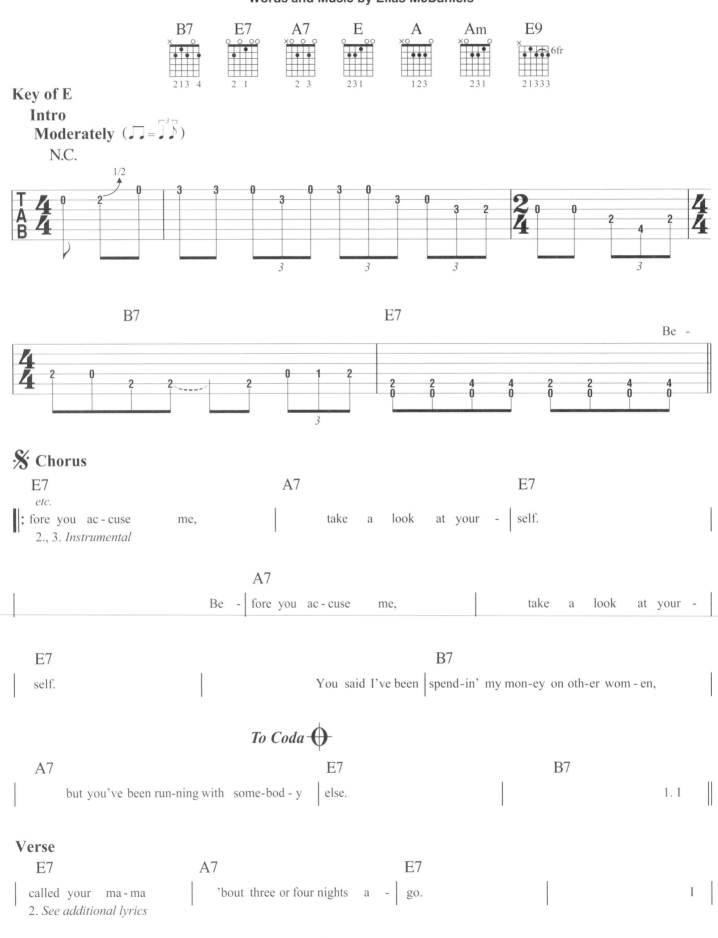

Key of E

Intro

Moderately

N.C.

S **Chorus**

E7   A7   E7

etc.

‖: fore you ac-cuse   me,   take   a   look   at   your - |self.

2., 3. Instrumental

A7

Be - |fore you ac-cuse   me,   take   a   look   at   your -

E7   B7

self.   You said I've been |spend-in' my mon-ey on oth-er wom - en,

To Coda ⊕

A7   E7   B7

but you've been run-ning with some-bod - y |else.   1. I

Verse

E7   A7   E7

called your ma-ma   'bout three or four nights a - |go.   I

2. See additional lyrics

A7   **E7**

| called your ma-ma | 'bout three or four nights a - | go. | | Your |

B7   **A7**   **B7**

| ma-ma said, "Son,   don't | call my daugh-ter no more!" | | Be - ‖

Chorus

E7   **A7**   **E7**

| fore you ac - cuse   me, | take a look at your - | self. | |

                                A7

| Be - | fore you ac - cuse   me, | take a look at your - |

E7   **B7**

| self. | | You said I'm | spend-in' my mon-ey on oth-er wom - en, |

                                              1.   2.

D.S. al Coda

A7   **E7**   **B7**   **B7**

| been tak-in' mon-ey from some-one else. | | :‖ | ‖

⊕ Coda

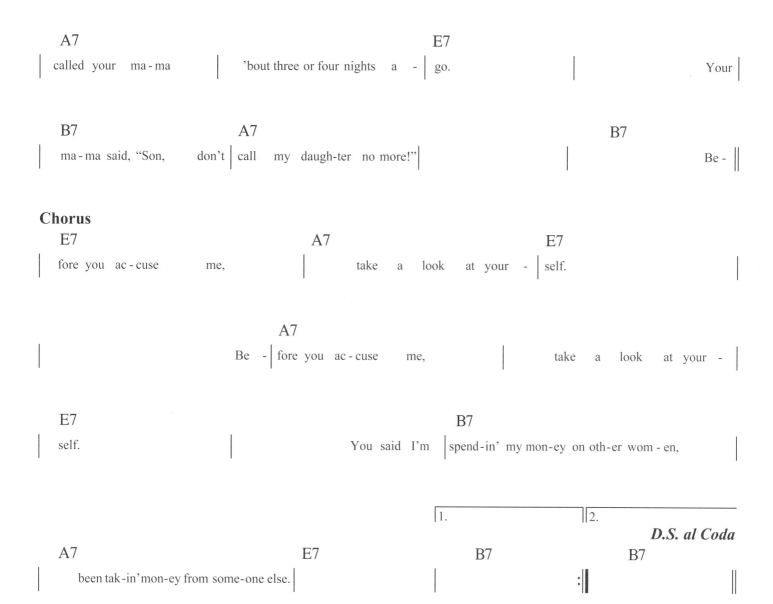

E E7   A   Am   E   B7 E   E9

Additional Lyrics

2. Come back home, baby.
   Try my love one more time.
   Come on back home, baby.
   Try my love one more time.
   You know I don't know when to quit you.
   I think I'll lose my mind.

Boogie Chillen No. 2

Words and Music by John Lee Hooker and Bernard Besman

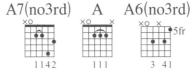

A7(no3rd)   A   A6(no3rd)

Key of A

Intro

Fast

A7(no3rd)

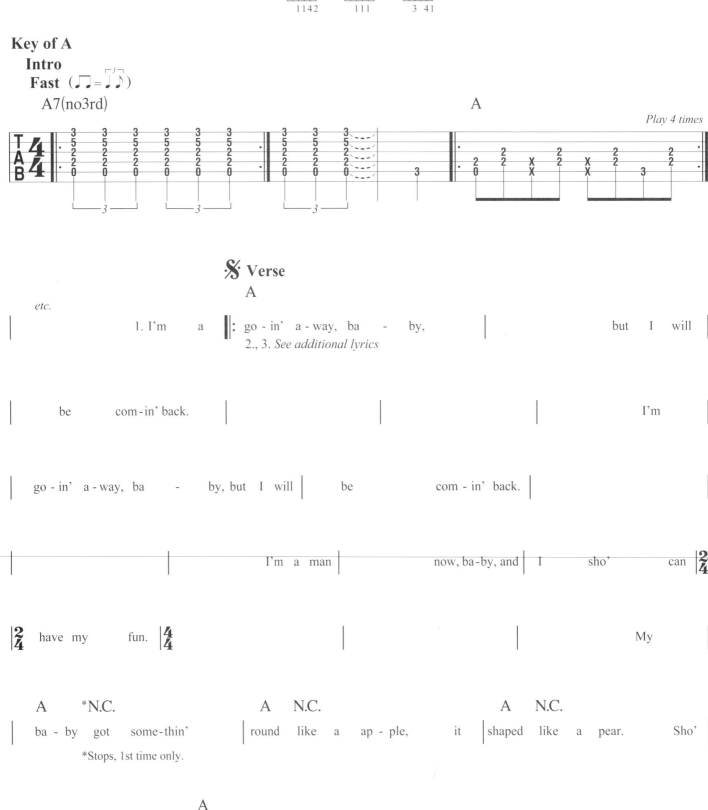

Play 4 times

A

𝄋 Verse

A

etc.

1. I'm a ‖: go - in' a - way, ba - by,   but I will

2., 3. *See additional lyrics*

be com - in' back.   I'm

go - in' a - way, ba - by, but I will | be com - in' back. |

I'm a man   now, ba-by, and | I sho' can |2/4

2/4 have my fun. |4/4   My

A   *N.C.   A N.C.   A N.C.

| ba - by got some-thin' | round like a ap - ple, it | shaped like a pear. Sho'

*Stops, 1st time only.

A

| now, babe. My ba | - by got some-thin', | my ba | - by got some-thin',

my ba - by got some-thin', man,   that I sho' do love.

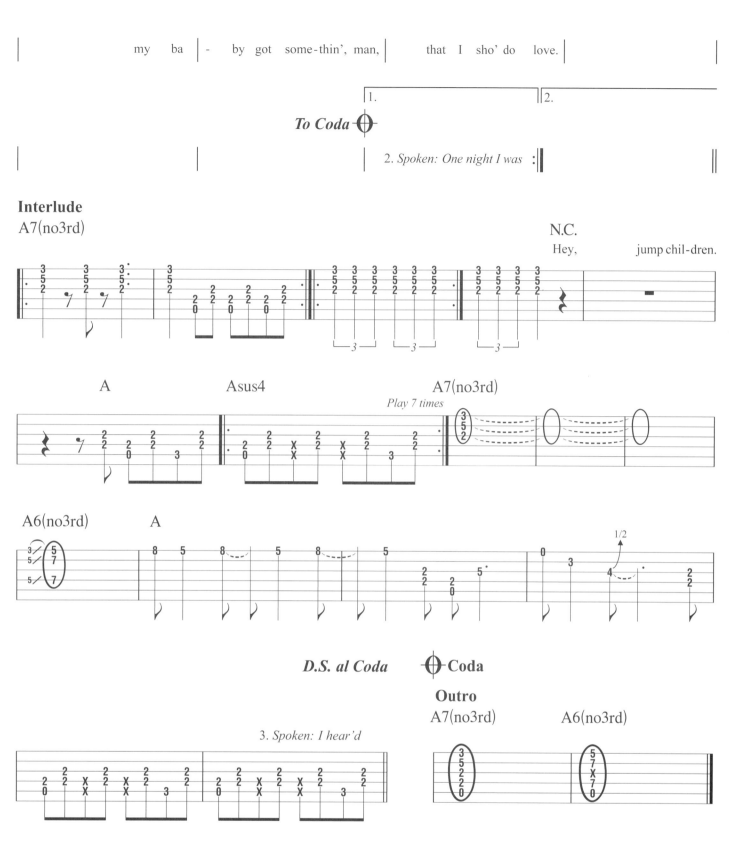

To Coda

2. *Spoken: One night I was*

Interlude

A7(no3rd)   N.C.
          Hey,   jump chil-dren.

A   Asus4   A7(no3rd)
                    Play 7 times

A6(no3rd)   A

D.S. al Coda   **Coda**

Outro
A7(no3rd)   A6(no3rd)

3. *Spoken: I hear'd*

Additional Lyrics

2. *Spoken:* One night I was laying down.
   I hear'd mama and poppa talkin'.
   I hear'd poppa tell mama, "Let that boy boogie woogie.
   He's a man now. Let him have his fun.
   You can't hold him down all the time."
   Sung: And I felt so good, went on boogie woogiein' just the same.

3. *Spoken:* I hear'd mama tell poppa again,
   "Why you so cruel on the boy?"
   "I don't know; in my days, boys didn't go around
   When they was eighteen and nineteen years old."
   But I hear'd her tell poppa, "That boy's a man, now."
   Sung: And I felt so good, went on boogiein' all night long.

Boom Boom

Words and Music by John Lee Hooker

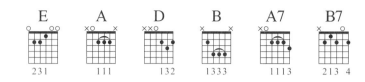

Key of E
Intro

Moderately fast

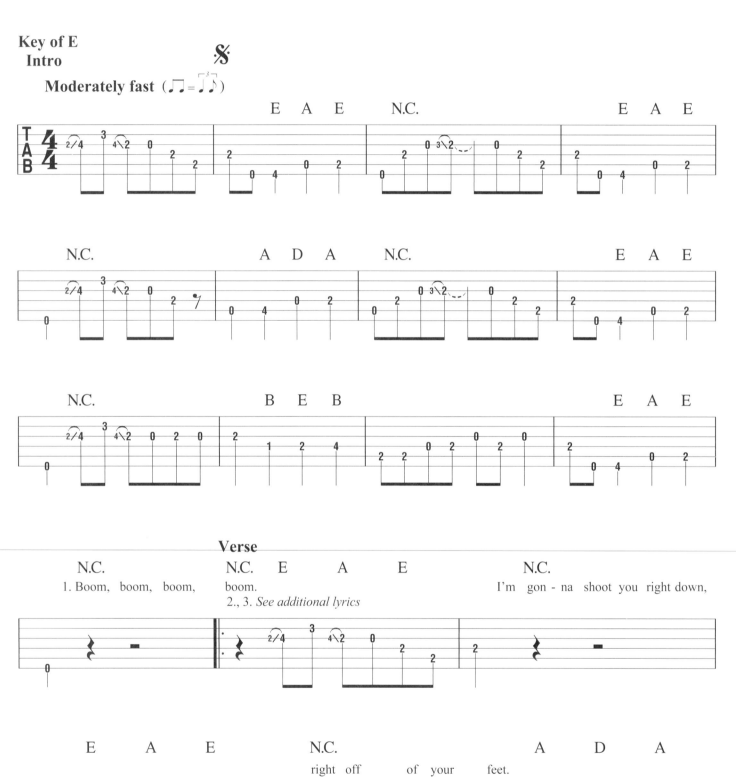

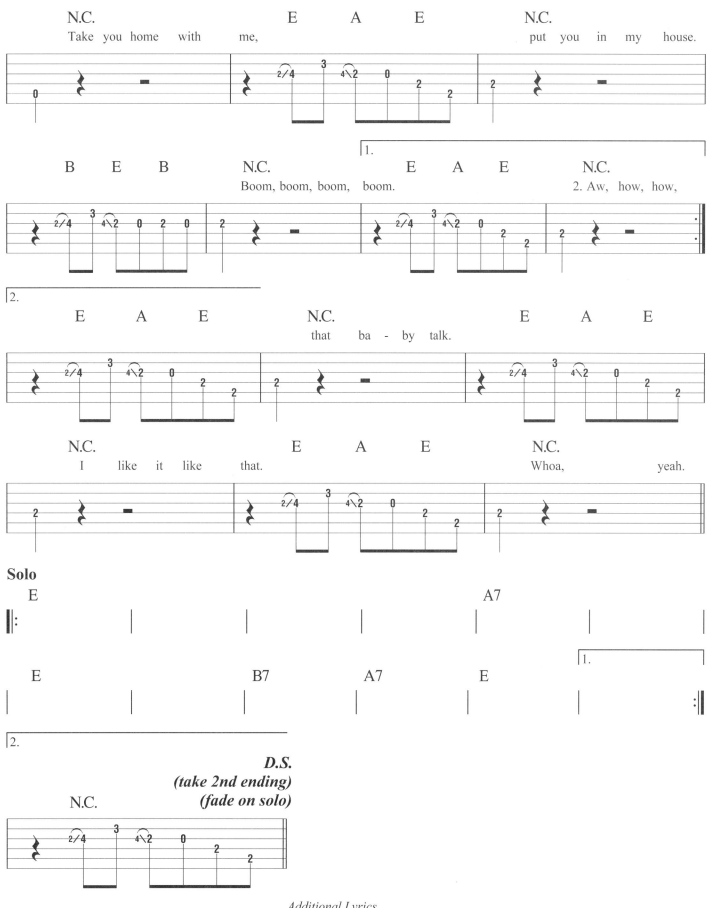

Additional Lyrics

2. Aw, how, how, how.
   Mm,
   Mm, mm, mm, mm.
   I love to see you strut
   Up and down the floor.
   When you're talkin' to me,

3. Won't you walk that walk
   And talk that talk?
   And whisper in my ear,
   Tell me that you love me.
   I love that talk
   When you talk like that.
   You knocks me out,
   Right off of my feet.
   Whoo, ho, ho, ho.

Born in Chicago

Words and Music by Nick Gravenites

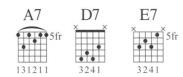

Key of A
Intro
Fast

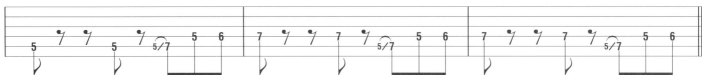

Verse
w/ Intro riff

A7

‖: in Chi - ca - go | in nine-teen and for - ty one. |

2., 4., 6. *See additional lyrics*
3., 5. *Instrumental*

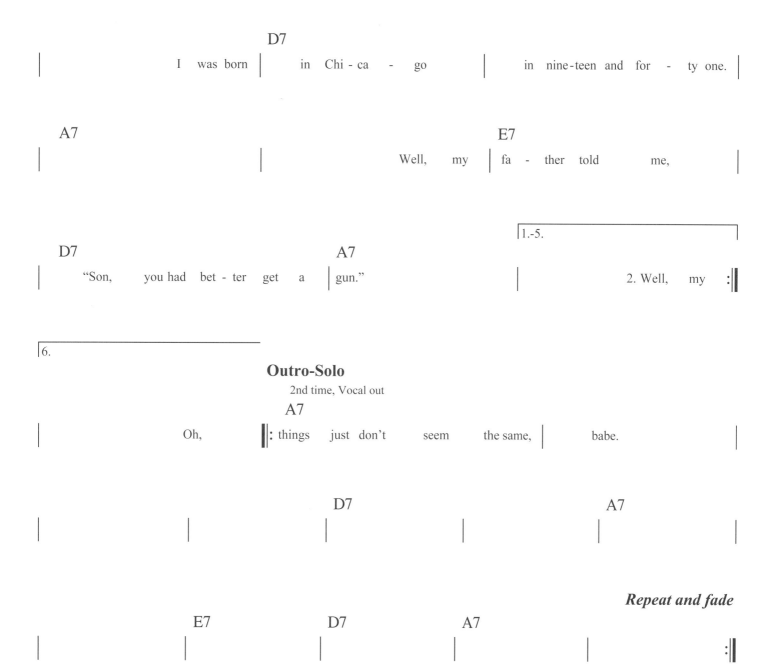

Additional Lyrics

2. Well, my first friend went down when I was seventeen years old.
   Well, my first friend went down when I was seventeen years old.
   Well, there's one thing I could say about that boy.
   He got bold.

4. Well, my second friend went down when I was twenty-one years of age.
   Well, my second friend went down when I was twenty-one years of age.
   Well, there's one thing I could say about that boy.
   He got brave.

6. Well, now, rules are alright if there's someone left to play the game.
   Well, now, rules are alright if there's someone left to play the game.
   All my friends are goin',
   And things just don't seem the same.

Born Under a Bad Sign

Words and Music by Booker T. Jones and William Bell

Bridge

G#7   A7   G#7   G7   F#7   F7   F#7   G7

know if it was-n't for bad   luck,   I would-n't have no kind of luck.

G#7   A7   G#7   G7   F#7 N.C.

If it was-n't for real   bad luck,   I would-n't have   no luck at all.

Verse

C#7   C#7

                            4. You know, wine   and wom-en

is all I crave.   A big   leg wom-an gon-na car - ry me

D.S. al Coda   ⊕ **Coda**   *Repeat and fade*

                       Outro-Solo

                       C#7

to my grave.

Additional Lyrics

2. I can't read; I didn't learn how to write.
    My whole life has been one big fight.

Come On in My Kitchen

Words and Music by Robert Johnson

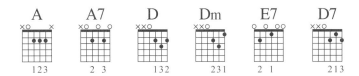

Key of A

Intro

Moderately slow

A   A7 D Dm   A E7

1. Ah, the wom-an I

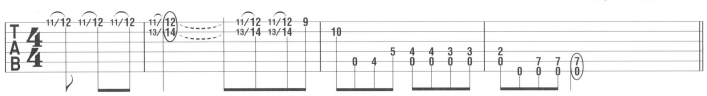

𝄋 Verse

A

‖: love   took from my best | friend.   Some jok-er got |

2., 3., 4. *See additional lyrics*

D7   A

| luck - y,   stole her back a - | gain.   You bet-ter come | on   in my kitch - |

4th time, to Coda ⊕

E7   A   D7

| en.   Babe,   it's | go - in' to be   rain - in' out - doors. |

1.

A

2. Ah,   she's

4. Win-ter time's

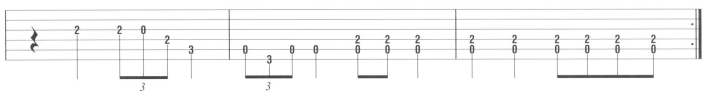

2.

Bridge

A7

Spoken: Oh, can't you hear the wind howl - in'?

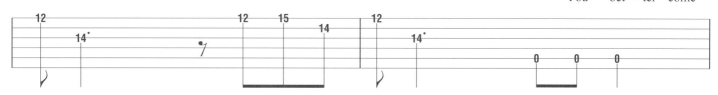

You bet - ter come

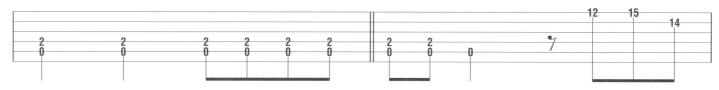

| on | in my kitch - en. | Babe, it's | go - in' to be rain - in' out - doors. |

D.S. al Coda
(take repeat)

A

3. When a wom-an gets in

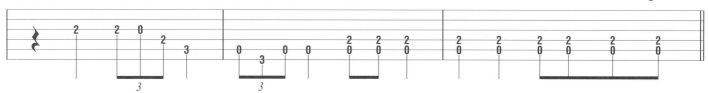

 Coda

A   E7   A

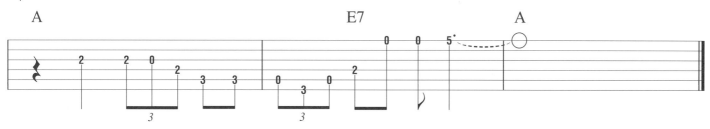

Additional Lyrics

2. Ah, she's gone. I know she won't come back.
I've taken the last nickel out of her nation sack.
You better come on in my kitchen.
Babe, it's goin' to be rainin' outdoors.

3. When a woman gets in trouble, ev'rybody throws her down.
Lookin' for her good friend, none can be found.
You better come on in my kitchen.
Babe, it's goin' to be rainin' outdoors.

4. Winter time's comin', it's gon' be slow.
You can't make the winter, babe, that's dry long so.
You better come on in my kitchen
'Cause it's goin' to be rainin' outdoors.

Crosscut Saw

Words and Music by R.G. Ford

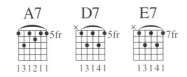

A7   D7   E7

Key of A
Intro-Solo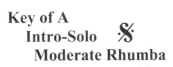
Moderate Rhumba

Bass arr. for gtr.

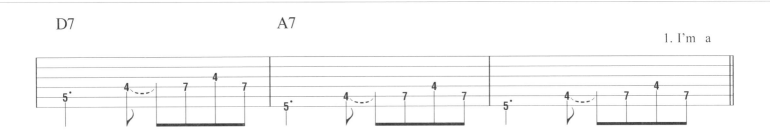

1. I'm a

Verse

A7

| cross - cut saw, | ba - by, just drag me a-cross | your log. |

 3. *Intrumental*

D7

| You know I'm a | cross-cut saw, | | just drag me a-cross your |

A7   E7

| log. | | I'll cut your | wood so eas - y for you, |

D7   A7

| you can't help but say, "Hot | dog." | 2. Now, some ‖

Verse

A7

| call me Wood - chop-pin' Sam, some | call me Wood - cut-tin' Jim. The |
4. *See additional lyrics*

| last girl I cut the wood for, you know, she | wants me back a - gain. I'm a |

D7   A7

| cross - cut saw, | just drag me a-cross your | log. |

E7

| I'll cut your | wood so eas - y for you, |

2nd time, D.S. and fade

D7   A7

| you can't help but say, "Hot | dog." | :‖

Additional Lyrics

4. I got a double bladed ax that really cuts good.
But I'm a crosscut saw, just bury me in your wood.
I'm a crosscut saw, baby, just drag me across your log.
I'll cut your wood so easy for you, woman,
You can't help but say, "Hot dog."

Dust My Broom

Words and Music by Elmore James and Robert Johnson

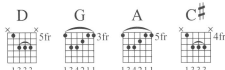

Key of D

Intro

Moderately

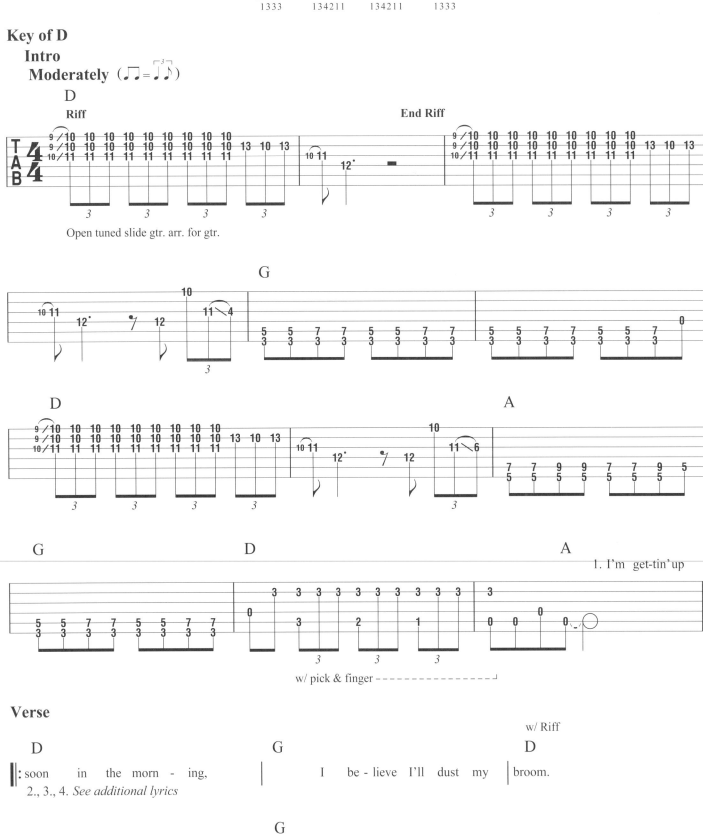

Open tuned slide gtr. arr. for gtr.

w/ pick & finger

Verse

w/ Riff

D	G	D
:soon in the morn - ing,	I be - lieve I'll dust my	broom.
2., 3., 4. *See additional lyrics*		

	G	
I'm get-tin' up	soon in the morn - ing.	I be - lieve I'll dust my

w/ Riff

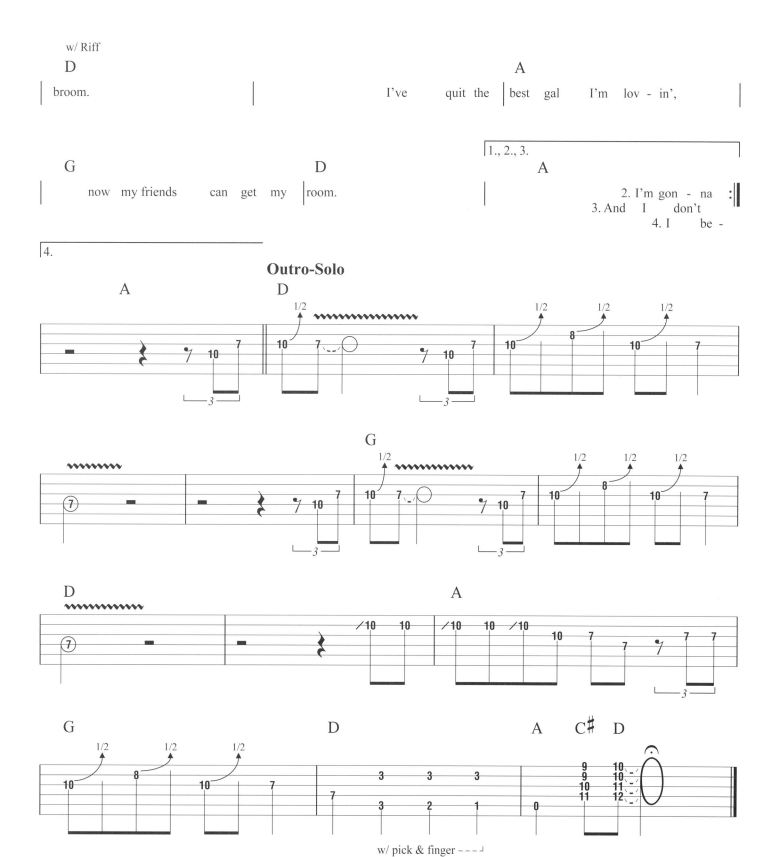

Outro-Solo

w/ pick & finger ---

Additional Lyrics

2. I'm gonna write a letter, telephone every town I know.
   I'm gonna write a letter, telephone every town I know.
   If I don't find her in Mississippi, she's over in West Memphis I know.

3. And I don't want no woman want every downtown man she meets.
   No, I don't want no woman want every downtown man she meets.
   Means she's a no good doney, they shouldn't 'low her on the street.

4. I believe, I believe my time ain't long.
   I believe, I believe my time ain't long.
   I ain't gonna leave my baby and break up my happy home.

Easy Baby

Words and Music by Willie Dixon

Key of Bm

Intro
Slow

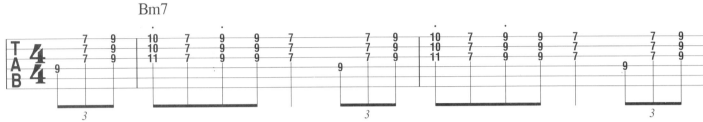

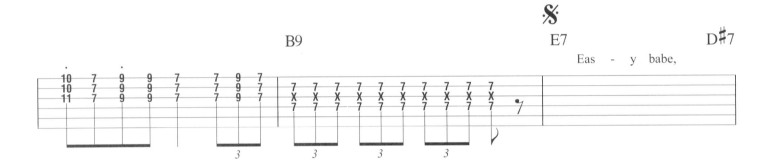

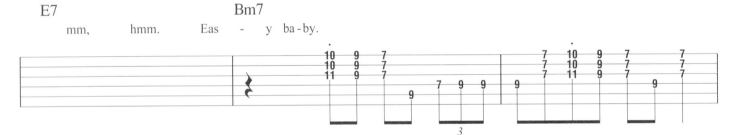

F#7 Eas - y   ba - by,

F7   E7   let me love you   night

To Coda

Bm7   and day.

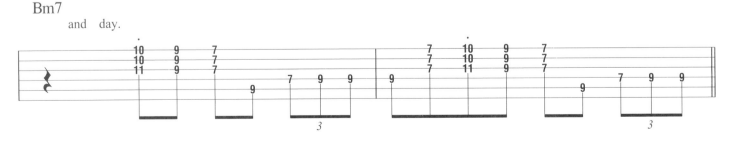

Verse

w/ Intro riff

Bm7

1. You don't have to work all day. Just make love to
2. *See additional lyrics*

                                         E7   **D#7**

me and say: Eas - y babe,

E7   **Bm7**

mm, hmm. Eas - y ba - by.

F#7   **F7**   **E7**

Eas - y ba - by, won't you love me night

Bm7

and day?

Interlude

Bm7

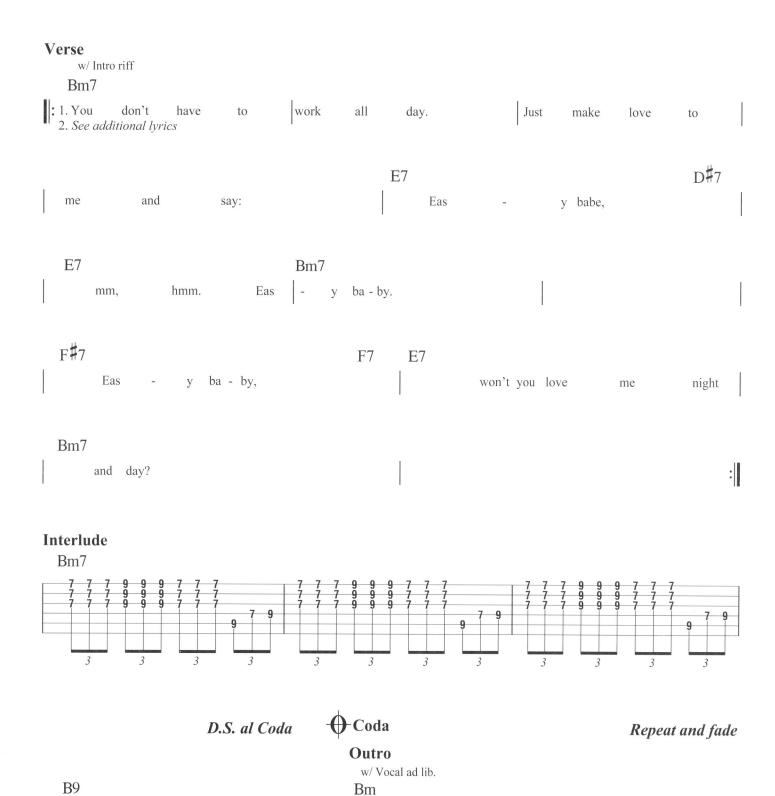

D.S. al Coda   ⊕ **Coda**   *Repeat and fade*

Outro

w/ Vocal ad lib.

B9   **Bm**

Additional Lyrics

2. You don't have to weep and moan.
   Just hold me, baby, in your arms.
   Easy baby, mm, hmm. Easy baby.
   Easy baby, let me love you night and day.

Further On Up the Road

Words and Music by Joe Veasey and Don Robey

Key of F

Intro
Moderately

F7

Horns arr. for gtr.

%: Verse

F7

1. Fur - ther on up the road, some - one's gon - na hurt you like

2., 5. *See additional lyrics*

you hurt me.

Bb7

Fur - ther on up the road,

F7

some - one gon - na hurt you like you hurt me.

Fur - ther on up the

To Coda ⊕

C7   Bb7 N.C.   F7

road,   ba - by, you just wait an' see.

1.   2.

N.C.   N.C.

2. You got to reap just what you :|| 3. Now you're laugh - ing, pret - ty ba -

Verse

F7

||: - by.   Some - day you gon - na be cry - in'.

4. *Instrumental*

B♭7

Now you're laugh - ing,   pret - ty | ba   -   by, | some, some - day   you   gon - na   be

F7   **C7**   **B♭7 *N.C.**

cry - in'. | Fur - ther on   up the | road, | you'll find out   I   was - n't |

*1st time only

1.   2.

D.S. al Coda

F7   **N.C.**   **N.C.**

ly - in'. | | :| 5. Fur - ther   on   up the road, ‖

⊕ Coda

Outro
w/ Vocal ad lib.

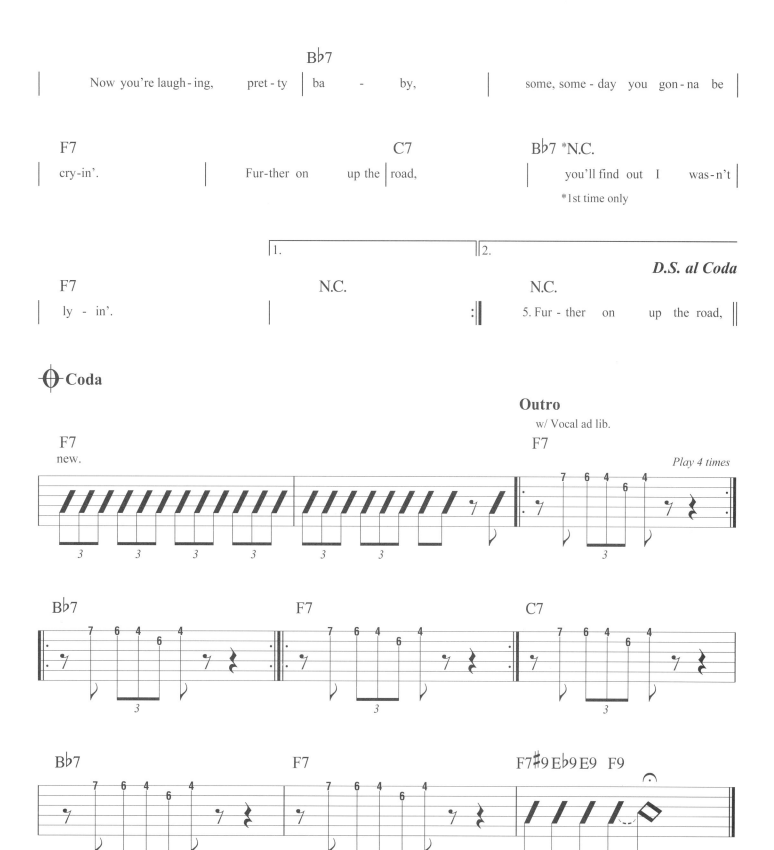

Additional Lyrics

2. You got to reap just what you sow. That ol' saying is true.
   You got to reap just what you sow. That ol' saying is true.
   Like you mistreat someone, someone's gonna mistreat you.

5. Further on up the road, when you're all alone 'n' blue,
   Further on up the road, when you're all alone 'n' blue,
   You gonna ask me to take you back, baby, but I'll have somebody new.

Honky Tonk

(Parts 1 & 2)

Words and Music by Berisford "Shep" Shepherd, Clifford Scott, Bill Doggett and Billy Butler

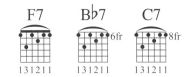

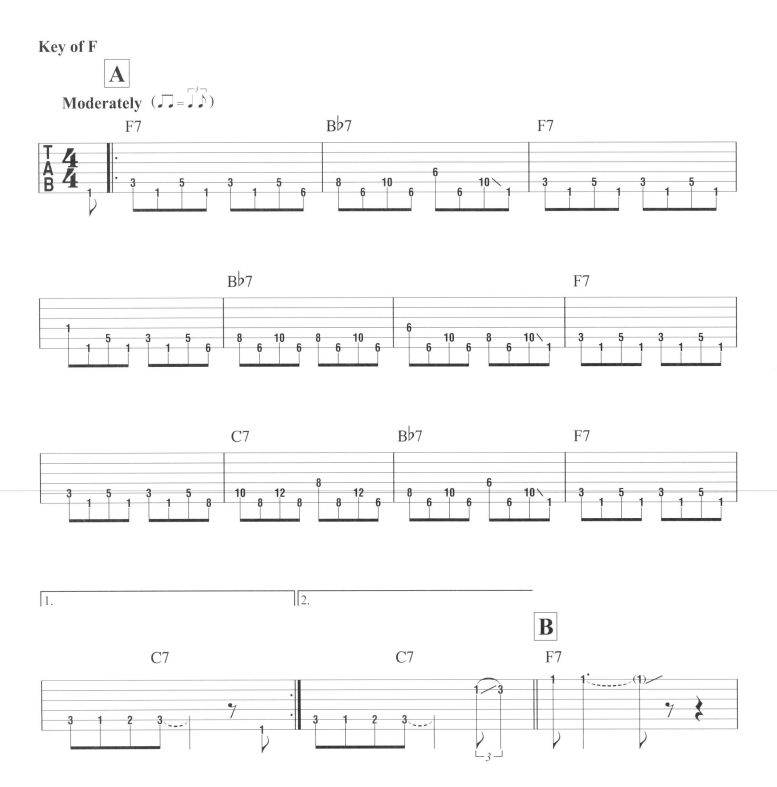

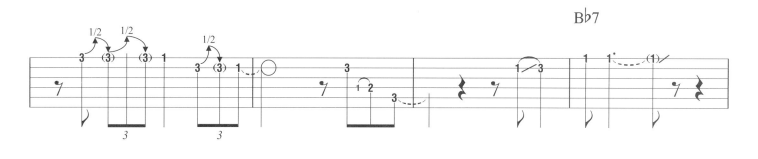

B♭7

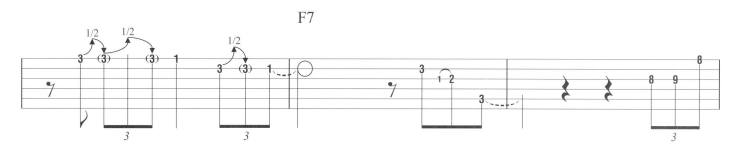

F7

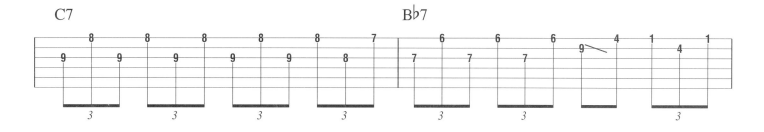

C7   B♭7

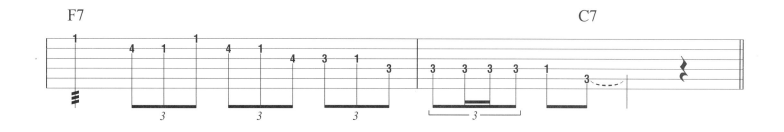

F7   C7

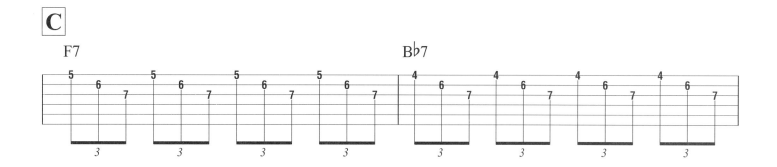

C

F7   B♭7

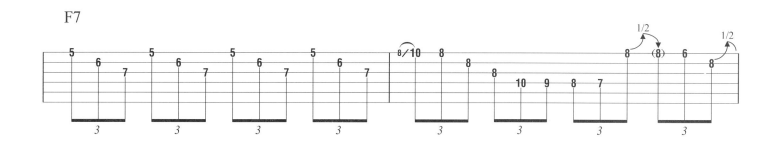

F7

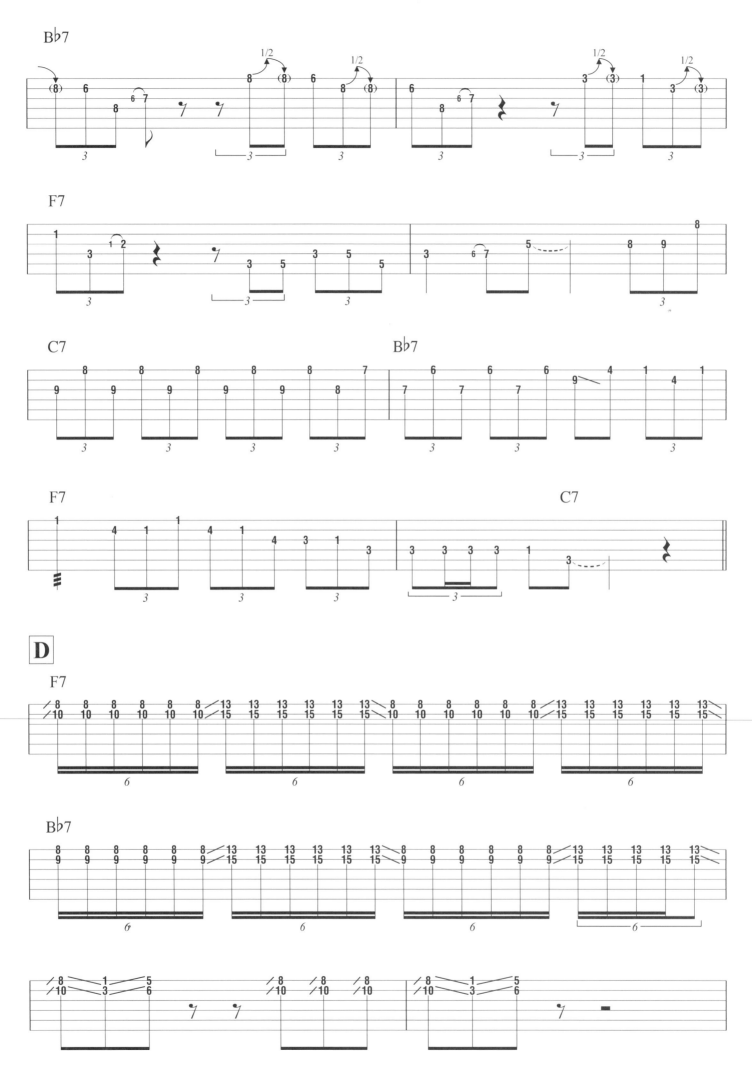

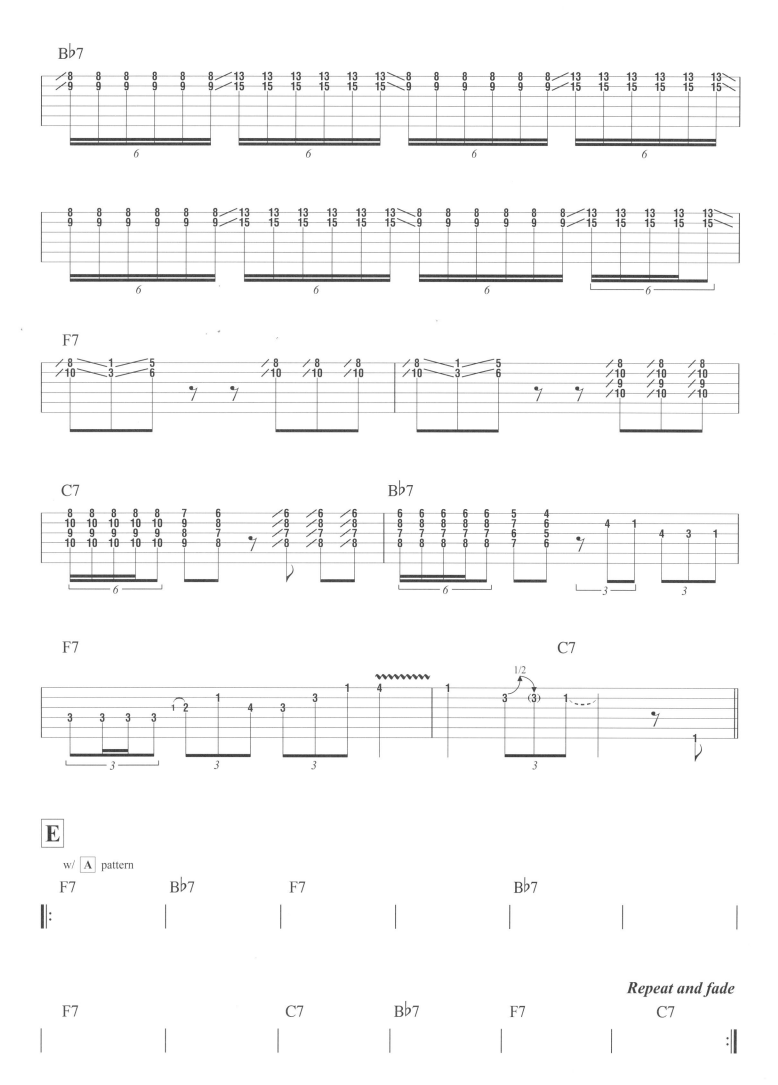

Hoodoo Man Blues

Words and Music by Junior Wells

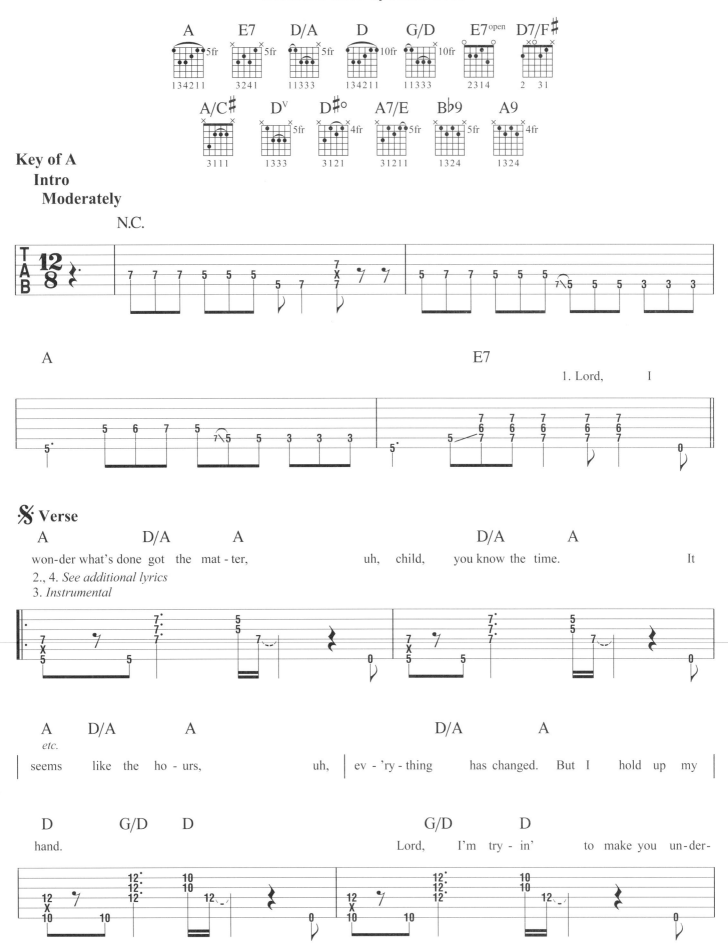

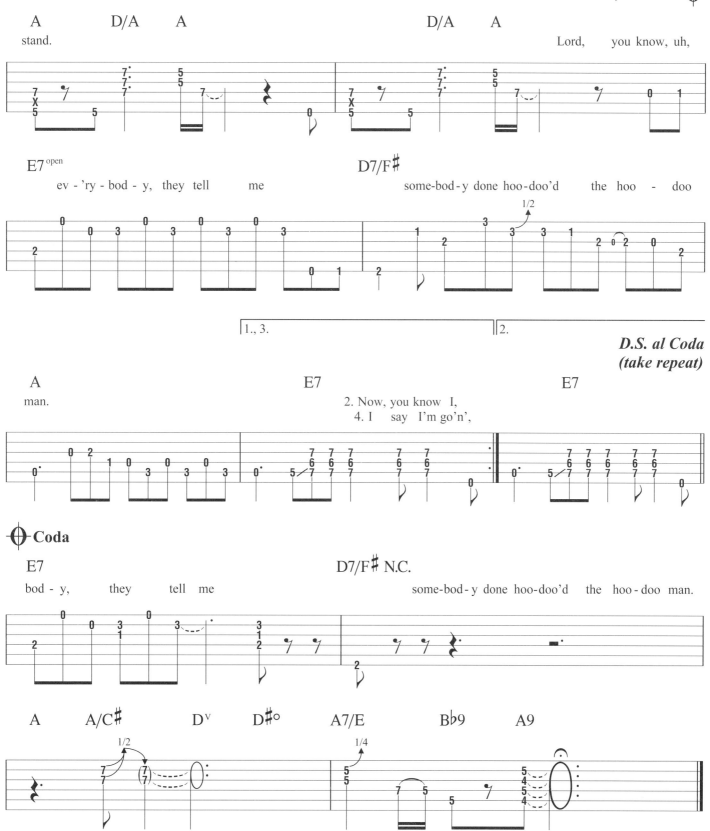

Additional Lyrics

2. Now, you know I, I buzzed your bell this mornin', baby,
   You had your elevator runnin' slow.
   I buzzed you bell, little girl, to take me up on the, uh, third floor.
   But I hold up my hand.
   Lord, I'm tryin' to make you understand.
   Lord, you know, uh, they tells the baby,
   That somebody done hoodoo'd the hoodoo man.
   Ha, ha, ha, ha, ha. Looky here, baby!

4. I say I'm gon', I tell you this time, babe,
   And I ain't gonna tell you no more.
   That next time I tell you, might have to, uh, let you go.
   But I hold up my hand.
   Lord, I'm tryin' to make her understand.
   Lord, you know, ev'rybody, they tell me
   Somebody done hoodoo'd the hoodoo man.

I Ain't Got You

Words and Music by Calvin Carter

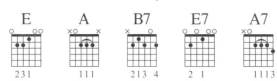

Key of E
Intro
Moderately fast

1. I got a

Verse
w/ Intro riff, sim.

El - do - ra - do Cad - il - lac | with the |spare tire on the back.
2. *See additional lyrics*

I got a |charge ac - count at Gold - blatt's, | but I

ain't got you. | 2. I got a | I got a

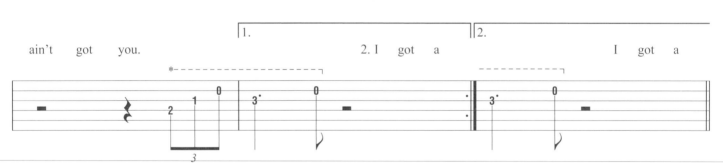

*Harmonica arr. for gtr.

Bridge

A
| tav - ern, a |pack - age store. I hit the |num - ber, four

| for - ty four, I got a |mo - jo, |don't you know? I'm

𝄋 **Verse**
w/ Intro riff, sim.

B7
| all dressed up 'n' no | place to go. 3. I got a ‖(4.) wom - en to the left of me.

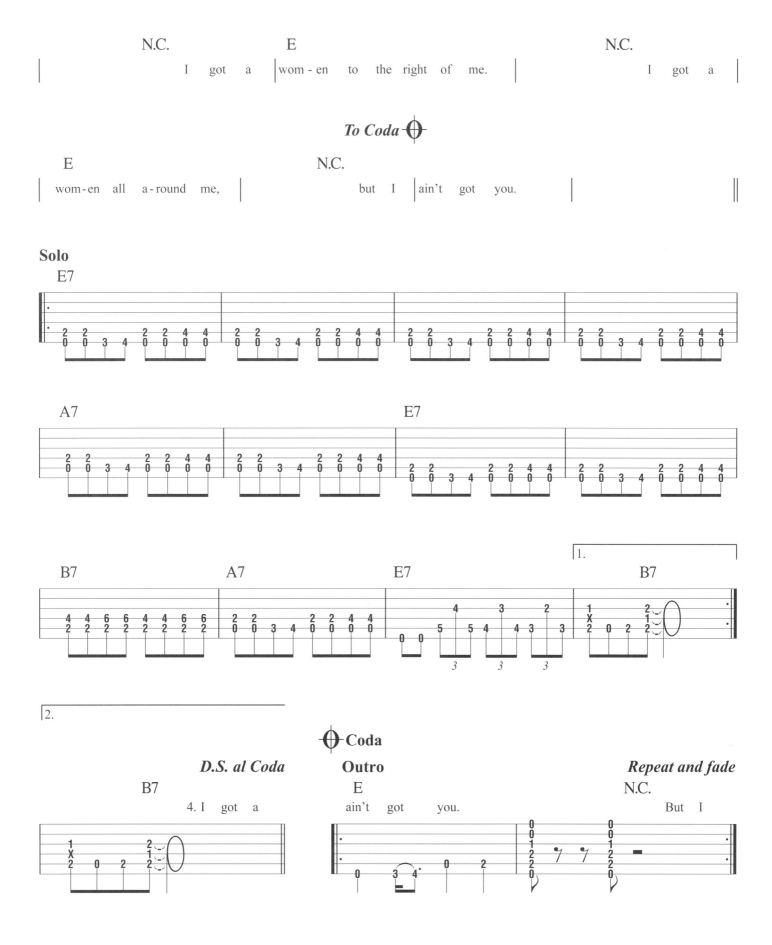

Additional Lyrics

2. I got a closet full of clothes.
   Don't matter where I go.
   You keep a ring in my nose,
   But I ain't got you.

I Wanna Put a Tiger in Your Tank

Words and Music by Willie Dixon

Bridge

A7   E7

| raise your | hood, I can | clean your coils, | |

A7   E7

| check your trans - | mis - sion then | e - ven the | oil. |

A7   E7

| I don't | care what the | peo - ple think. | I |

D.S. al Coda

B7   N.C.

| wan - na put a | ti - ger, you know, | in your tank. | 3. Your ‖

⊕ Coda

Solo

E7

| | ‖ | | | | | |

                                      A7

| | | | | | | |

             E7   B7   A7

| | | | | | | |

                      E7   B7

| | | | | | I ‖

Outro

E7

‖: wan - na put a | ti - ger | in your tank. | |

Repeat and fade

w/ Riff A

| | | | I :‖

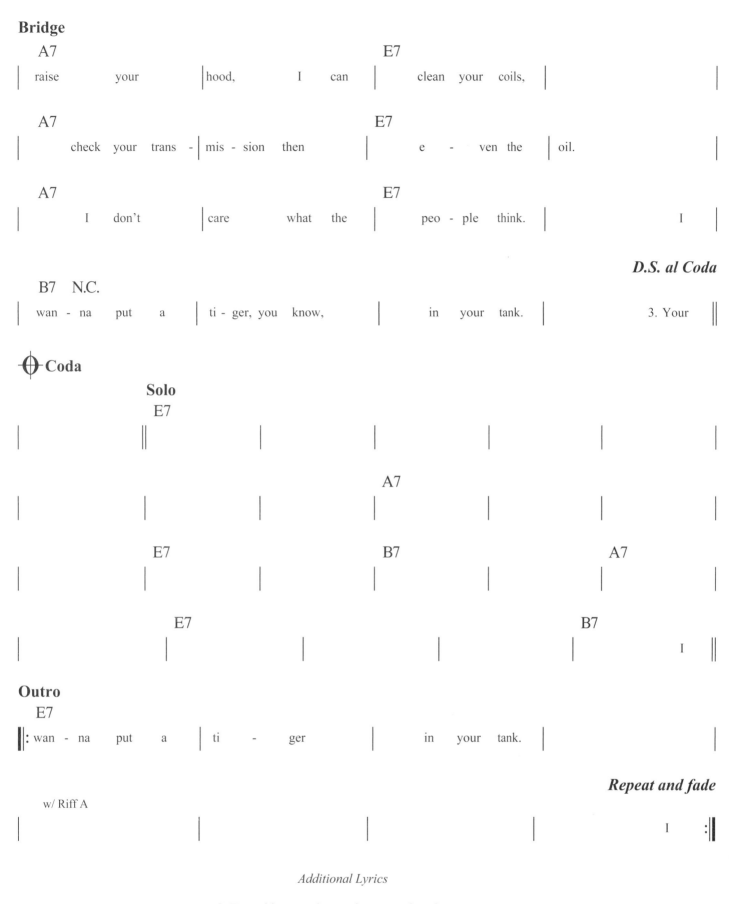

Additional Lyrics

2. Everything you do, you know you knocks me out.
   I want you to feel good where you can jump and shout.
   I have no money, you know, in the bank.
   I wanna put a tiger in your tank.

3. Your motor's puttin' and poppin' and missin', too.
   One thing left for you to do.
   If you give it a push and the car don't crank,
   I wanna put a tiger in your tank.

I'm Tore Down

Words and Music by Sonny Thompson

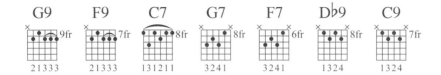

Key of C

Intro-Solo

Moderately fast

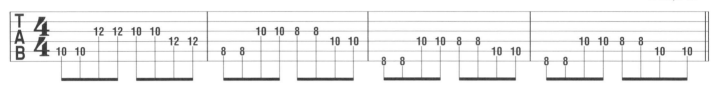

$\mathcal{S}\!\cdot\!\mathcal{S}$ **Chorus**

w/ Intro riff

C7

| tore down, | I'm | al - most lev - el with the | ground. | | Well, I'm |

F9　　　　　　　　　　　　　　　　　　　　**C7**

| tore down, | I'm | al - most lev - el with the | ground. | | Whyd' |

To Coda 2 ⊕

G7　　　　　　　**F7**　　　　　　　**C7**

| I feel like this when | my ba - by can't be found? | | 1. A well, I |

Verse

C7 N.C.　　　　**C7 N.C.**　　　　**C7 N.C.**　　　　**C7**

| went to the riv - er | to jump in. My | ba - by showed up and said, | "I will tell you when." Well, I'm |

Chorus

F9　　　　　　　　　　　　　　　　　　　　**C7**

| tore down, | I'm | al - most lev - el with the | ground. | | Whyd' |

G7　　　　　　　**F7**　　　　　　　**C7**

| I feel like this when | my ba - by can't be found? | | 2. I |

𝄋 Verse

C7 N.C.　　　　　　　　　　C7 N.C.　　　　　　　C7 N.C.

love　you　ba - by　with　all　my　heart　and　soul,　　　a　love　a　like　mine　a　will

3. *See additional lyrics*

C7 N.C.　　　　　　　　　　C7 N.C.　　　　　　　C7 N.C.

nev - er　grow　old.　　I　love　you　in　the　morn-ing　and　in　the　eve - nin' too,　　but

C7　N.C.　　　　　　　　　　C7

ev - 'ry　time　you　leave　me　I　get　mad　with　you.　　Well,　I'm

Chorus

F9　　　　　　　　　　　　　　C7

tore　down,　　I'm　al - most　lev - el　with　the　ground.　　　　　Whyd'

To Coda 1 ⊕

G7　　　　　　F7　　　　C7

I　feel　like　this　when　my　ba - by　can't　be found?

Solo

C7　　　　　　　　　　　　　　　　F7

𝄆

　　　　　C7　　　　　　　　　　G7　　　F7

|1.　　　　　|2.

D.S. al Coda 1　　⊕ *Coda 1*　　　　　*D.S.S. al Coda 2*

C7　　　　　　　　　　　　　　　　　C7

　　　　　　　　　　　𝄇　3. I　　　　　　　　　　Well, I'm

⊕ Coda 2

F7 N.C.　　　　　　　C7　　F7　　　　C7　　D♭9 C9

my　ba - by　can't　be found.

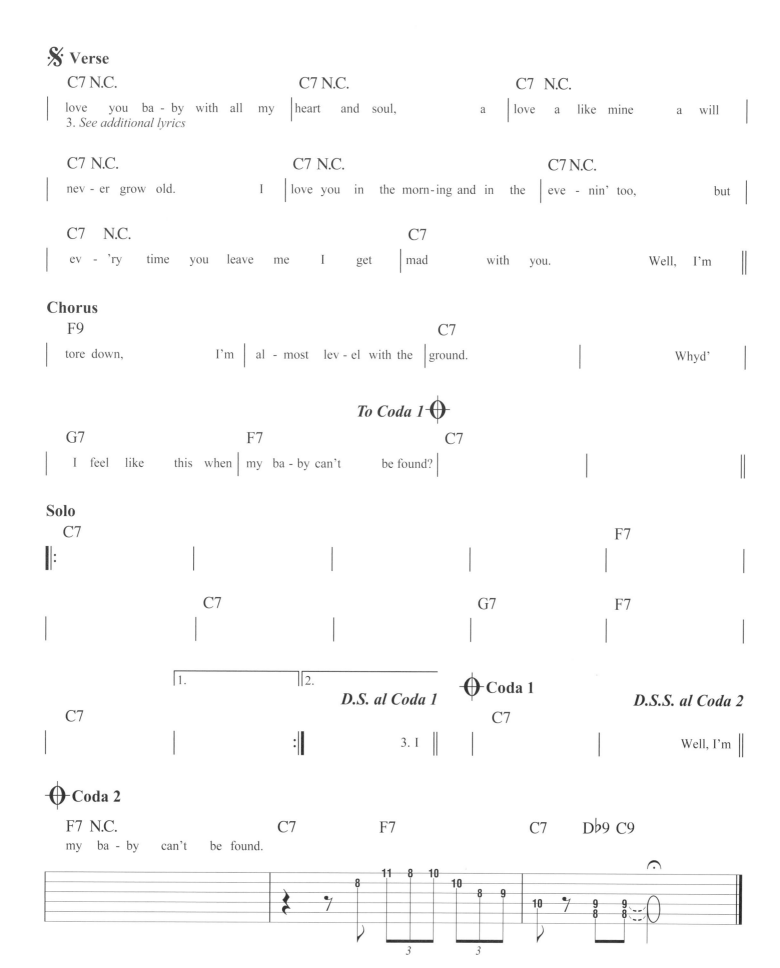

Additional Lyrics

3. I love you, baby, with all my might.
　A love like mine is outta sight.
　I'll lie for you if you want me to.
　I really don't believe your love is true.

I'm Your Hoochie Coochie Man

Words and Music by Willie Dixon

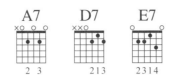

Key of A

Intro
Slow

A7 N.C.   A7 N.C.

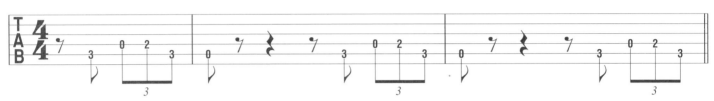

Verse

A7   N.C.   A7   N.C.

1. The gyp-sy wom-an told my moth-er,   be-fore   I   was born,
2., 3. *See additional lyrics*

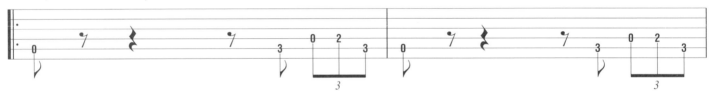

A7 N.C.   A7 N.C.

"I got a boy child's com-in',   he's gon' be a son of a gun.
etc.

A7 N.C.   A7 N.C.

He gon-na make pret-ty wom-ens   jump and shout.

A7 N.C.   A7

Then the world wan-na know,   what this all a-bout."   But you know I'm here.

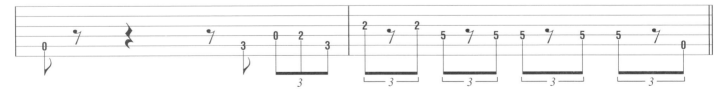

Chorus

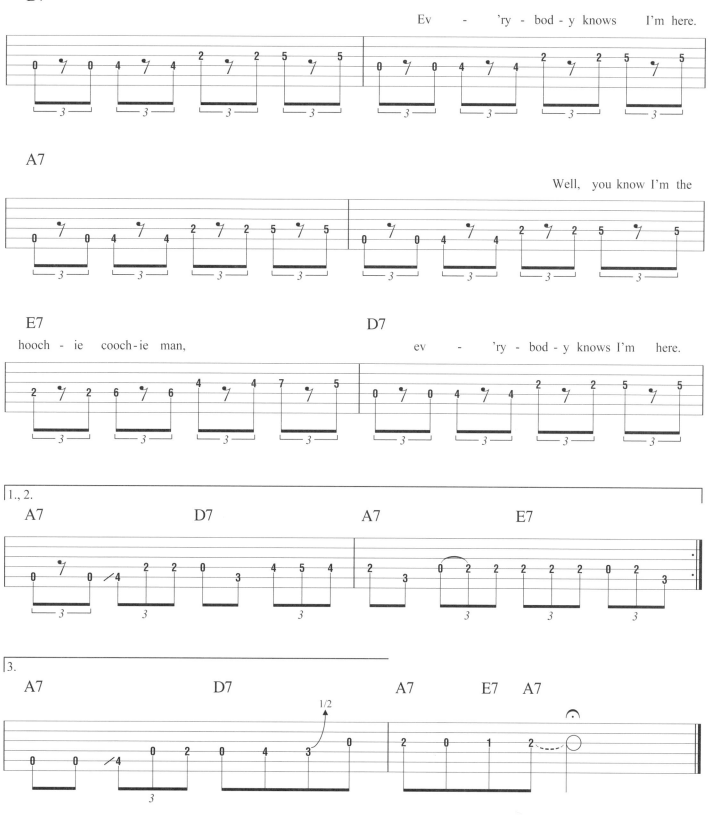

Additional Lyrics

2. I got a black cat bone, I got a mojo too,
   I got the John the Conquer'r root, I'm gonna mess with you.
   I'm gonna make you girls lead me by my hand,
   Then the world'll know the hoochie coochie man.

3. On the seventh hour, on the seventh day,
   On the seventh month, the seventh doctor say,
   "He was born for good luck, and that you'll see."
   I got seven hundred dollars, don't you mess with me.

If You Love Me Like You Say

Words and Music by Little Johnny Taylor

Key of C

Intro

Moderately

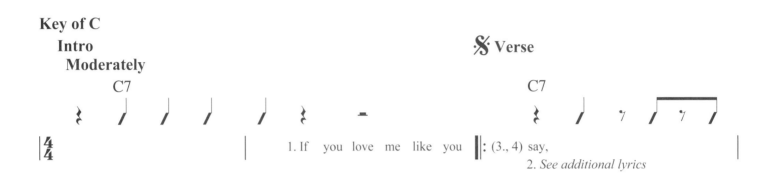

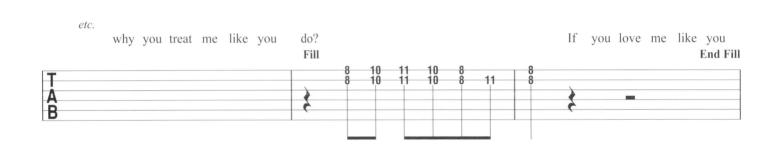

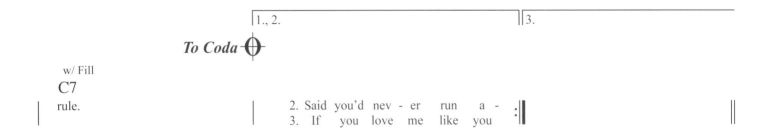

Solos

C7

‖: | | | |

F9   C7

| | | | |

G9   F9   C7   ⌐Open

| | | | :‖

⌐After solos   ⊕ **Coda**

                    D.S. al Coda   **Outro**

N.C.   N.C.   G13   G♭13

| 4. If you love me like you ‖ | Why, yah, yah, ‖ yah. |

                    w/ Fill

F13   C7   N.C.   G13   G♭13

| I'm cool,   I know the | rule. | Why, yah, yah, | yah. |

                    w/ Fill

F13   C7   N.C.

| I'm cool,   I know the | rule. | Yeah!   ‖

Additional Lyrics

2. Said you'd never run around, said you'd never stay out late.
   Said you'd never run around, baby, said you'd never stay out late.
   Let me tell you, pretty baby, I've got to set you straight.

Juke

Words and Music by Walter Jacobs

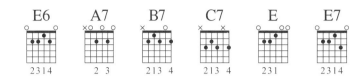

Key of E

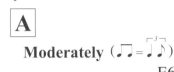

Moderately

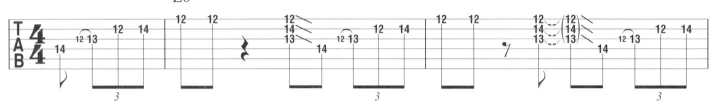

Harmonica & guitar arr. for gtr.

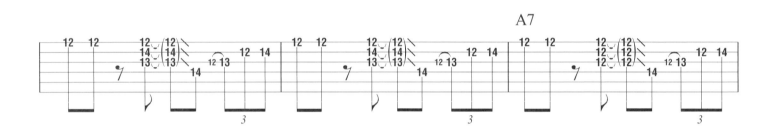

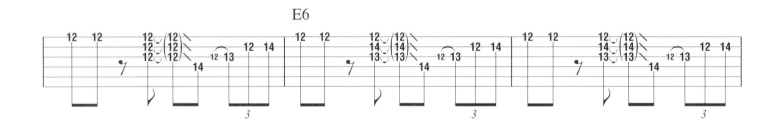

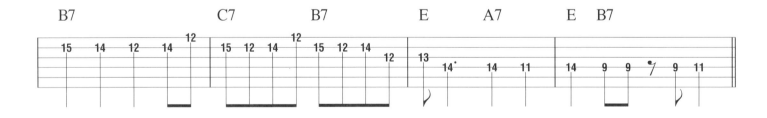

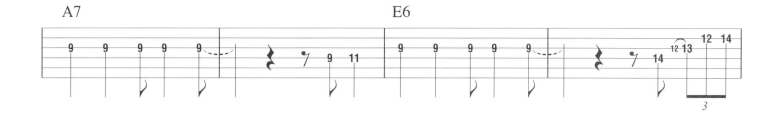

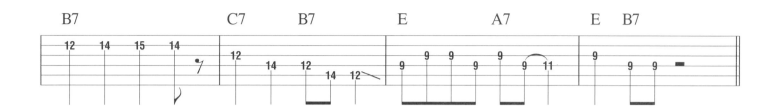

Solos

E6

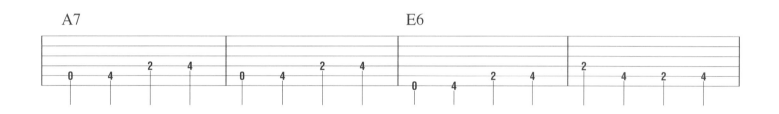

Guitar

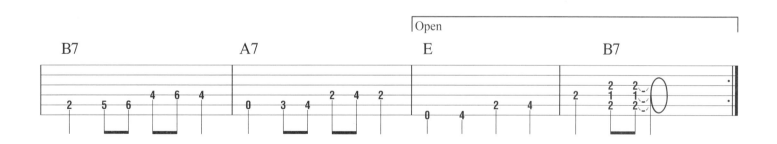

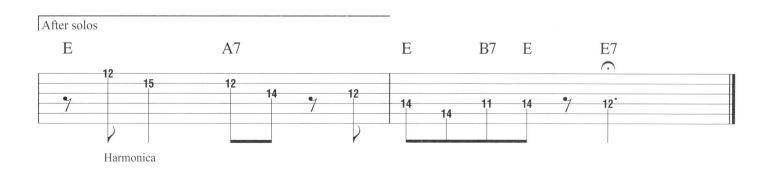

Harmonica

Just Your Fool

Words and Music by Walter Jacobs

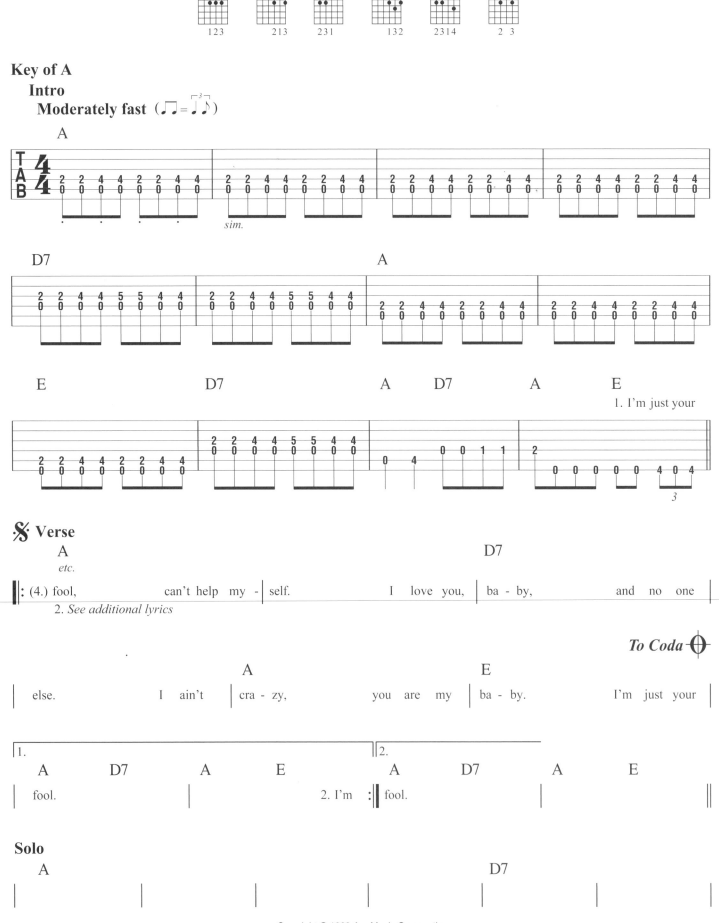

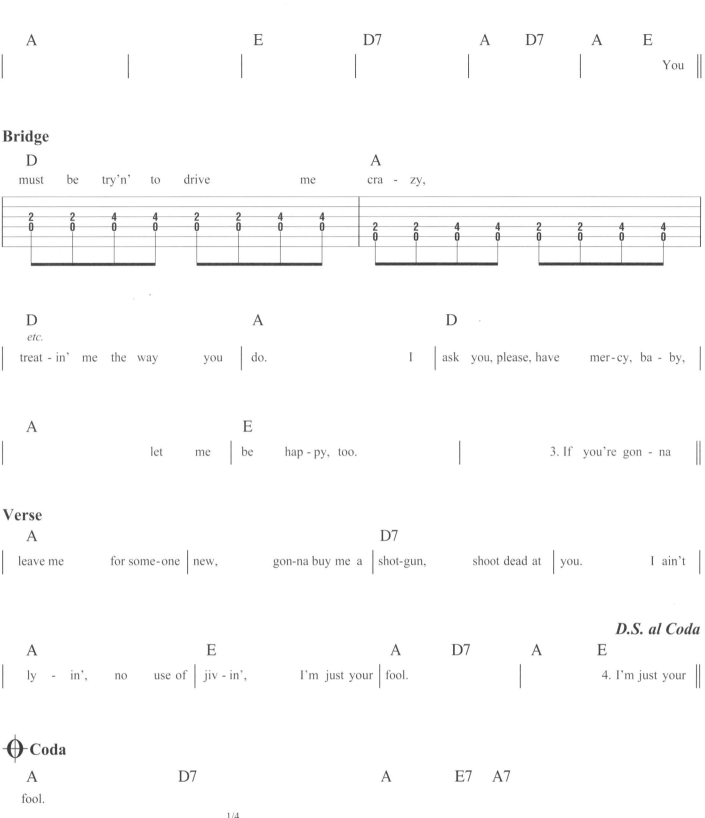

Additional Lyrics

2. I'm just your fool, I must confess,
   Still love you, baby, and take your mess.
   I ain't lyin', no use of jivin',
   I'm just your fool.

Killing Floor

Words and Music by Chester Burnett

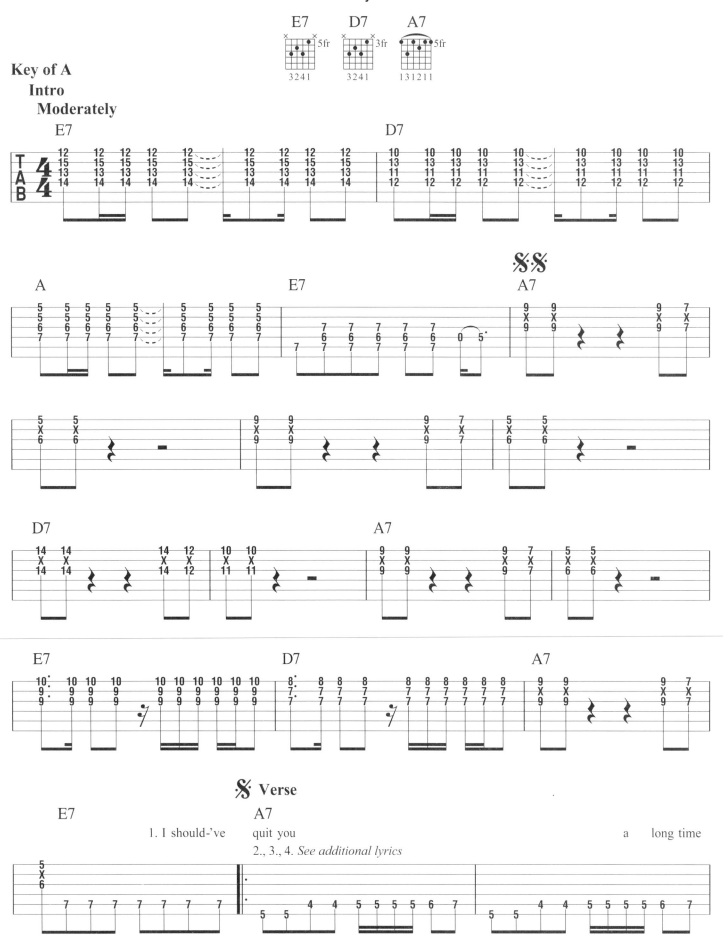

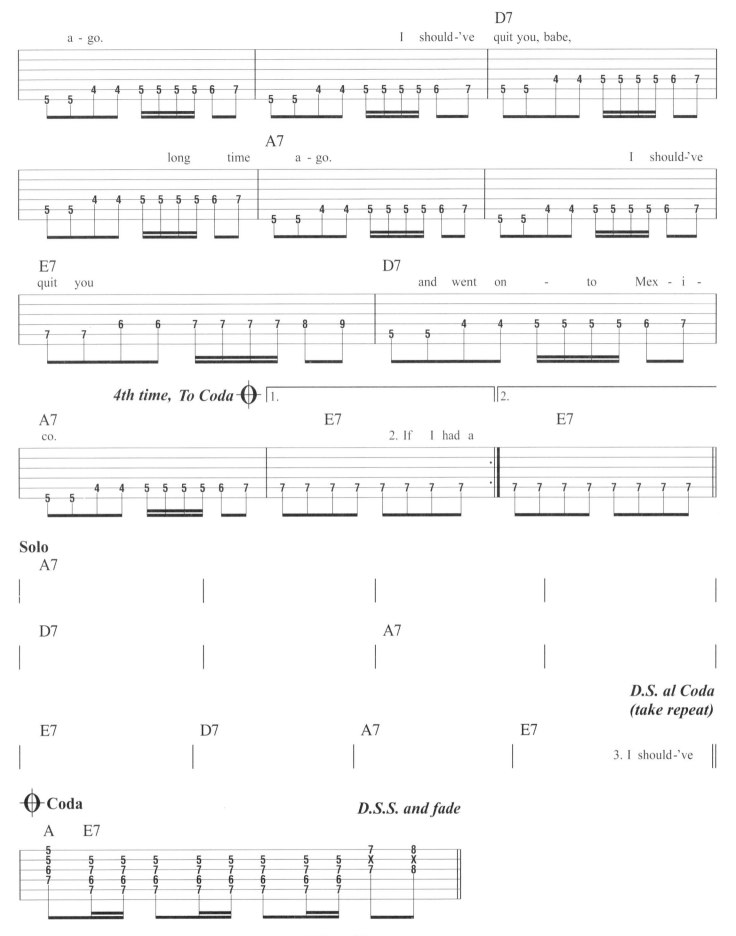

Additional Lyrics

2. If I had a followed my first mind.
   If I had a followed my first mind.
   I'd a been gone, it's my second time.

3. I should've went on when my friend come from Mexico at me.
   I should've went on when my friend come from Mexico at me.
   But no, I'm foolin' with you, baby, I let you put me on the killin' floor.

4. Lord knows, I should've been gone.
   Lord knows, I should've been gone.
   And I wouldn't a been here, down on the killin' floor.

Let the Good Times Roll

Words and Music by Sam Theard and Fleecie Moore

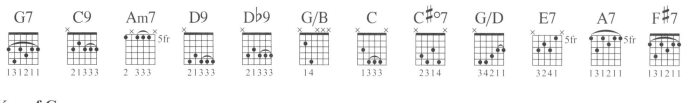

Key of G
Verse
Moderately

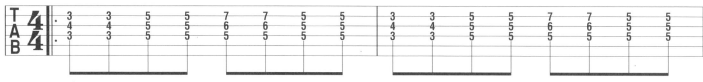

G7

1. Hey,   ev - 'ry - bod - y,   let's have some fun.
2., 3. *See additional lyrics*

Piano arr. for gtr.

You on - ly live but once,   and when you're dead   you're done.   Let the

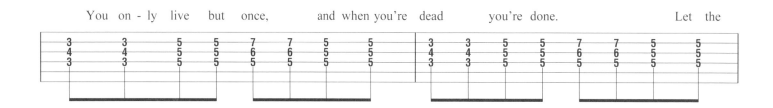

C9   G7

(4.) good times   roll,   let the   good times   roll.

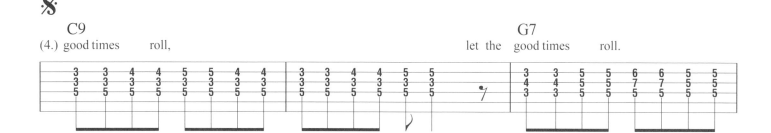

Am7   D9

Don't care if you're young or old.   Get to-geth-er and let the good times roll.

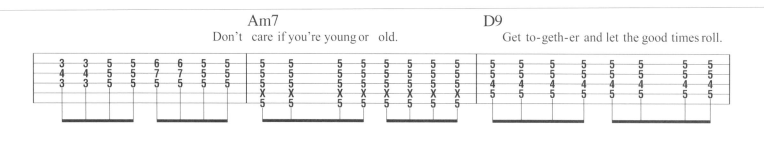

1., 2.   **3.**

To Coda ⊕

G7   C9   G7   D9   G7   D9

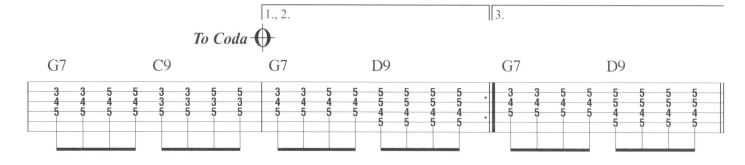

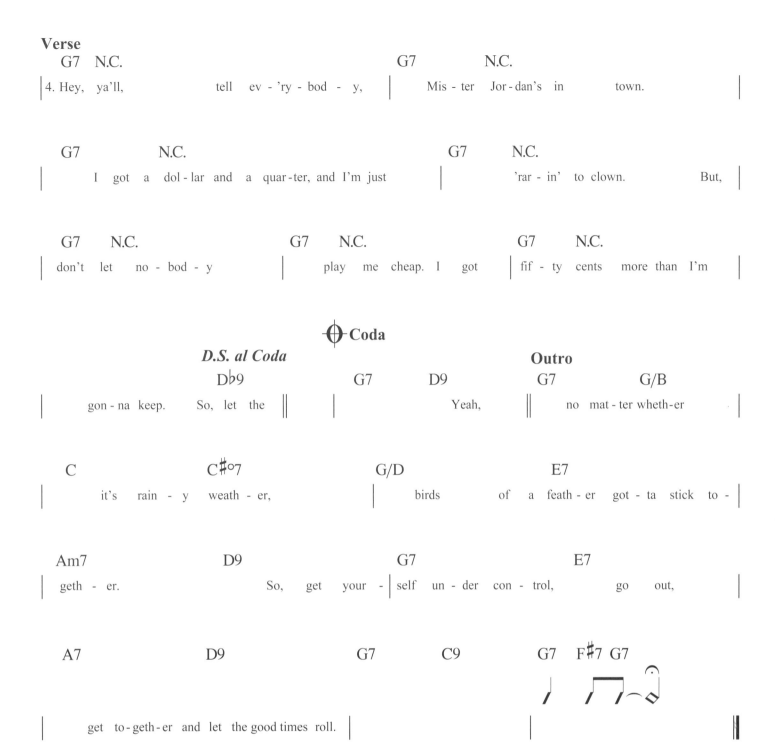

Additional Lyrics

2. Don't sit there mumblin' and talkin' trash.
 If you wanna have a ball you gotta go out and spend some cash.
 Let the good times roll, let the good times roll.
 Don't care if you're young or old.
 Get together and let the good times roll.

3. Hey, mister landlord, lock up all the doors.
 When the police comes around tell them the joint is closed.
 Let the good times roll, let the good times roll.
 Don't care if you're young or old.
 Go out and let the good times roll.

Little Red Rooster

Words and Music by Willie Dixon

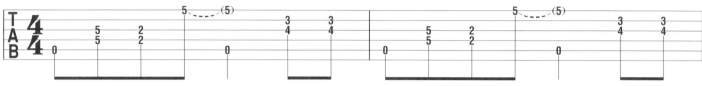

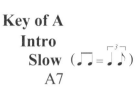

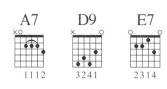

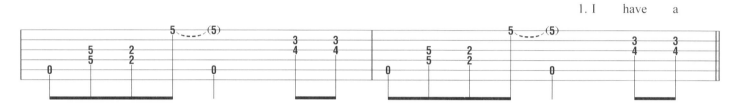

Slide gtr. arr. for gtr.

1. I have a

Verse

A7
etc.

‖: lit - tle red roost - er, | too la - zy to crow 'fore day. |

2., 3. *See additional lyrics*

D9

I have a | lit - tle red roost - er, | too la - zy to crow 'fore day.

A7   E7

Keep ev - 'ry-thing | in the barn - yard

1., 2.

D9   A7

up - set   in ev -'ry way. | 2. Oh, the :‖

3.

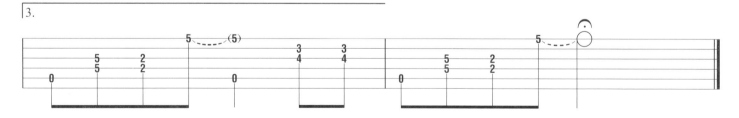

Additional Lyrics

2. Oh, the dogs begin to bark and the hounds begin to howl.
   Oh, the dogs begin to bark and the hounds begin to howl.
   Oh, watch out, strange kin people, 'cause the little red rooster's on the prowl.

3. If you see my little red rooster, please drive him home.
   If you see my little red rooster, please drive him home.
   There's been no peace in the barnyard since the little red rooster's been gone.

Pride and Joy

Written by Stevie Ray Vaughan

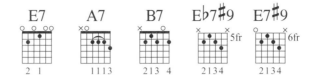

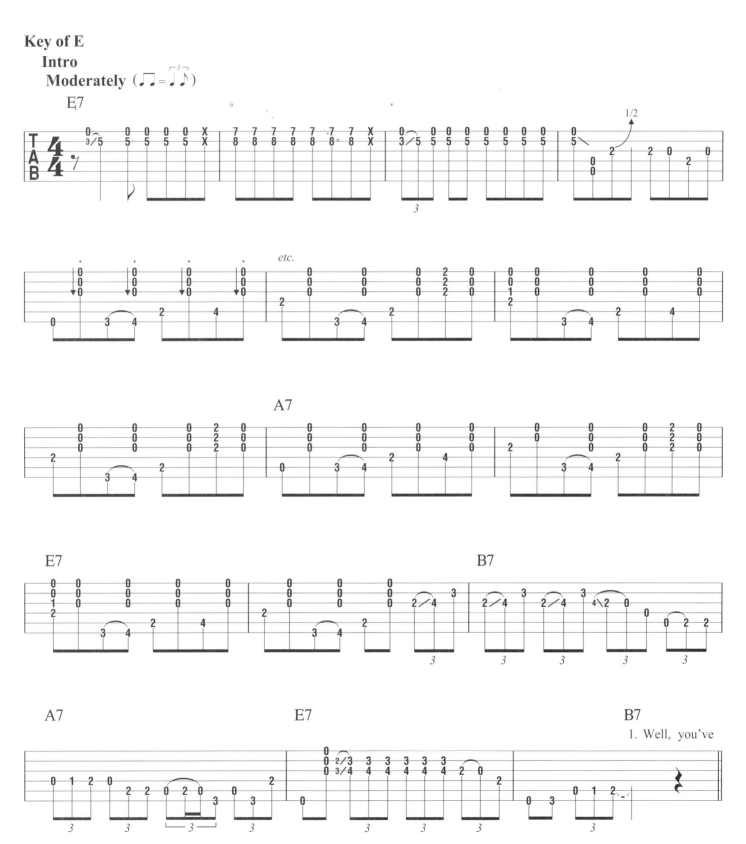

E7

‖: heard a - bout lov - in' giv - in' sight | to the blind. | My ba - by's lov - in' cause the sun

2., 5. *See additional lyrics*

6. *Instrumental*

A7

to shine. And she's my | sweet lit - tle thang, | she's my |

E7 | | B7

pride and joy. | She's my | sweet lit - tle ba - by, I'm

1.

To Coda 2

A7 | | E7 | B7

her lit - tle lov - er boy. | | 2. Yeah, I :‖

2.

𝄋 **Verse**

B7 | E7 N.C.

3. Yeah, I love my la - dy, she's long and lean.

4. *See additional lyrics*

E7 N.C. | E7 | A7

You mess with her, you'll see a man get - tin' mean. She's my sweet lit - tle thang,

etc. | E7 | B7

she's my | pride and joy. | She's my | sweet lit - tle ba - by, I'm

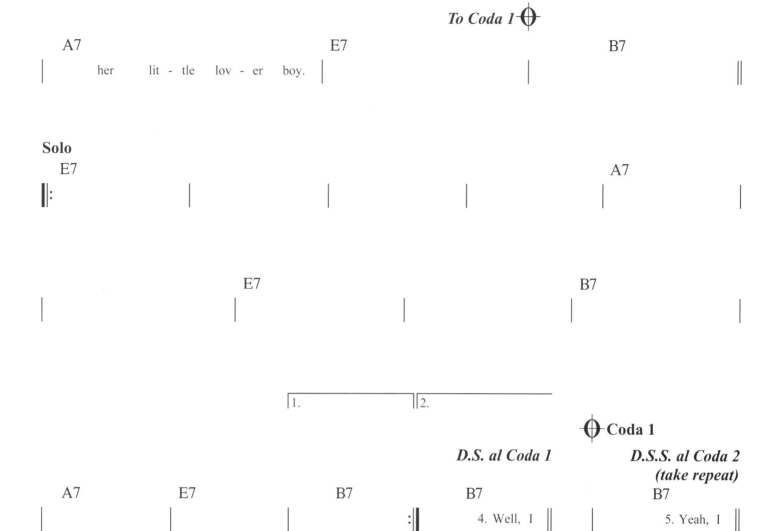

To Coda 1

A7   her lit - tle lov - er boy.   E7   B7

Solo

E7   A7

E7   B7

1.   2.

Coda 1

D.S. al Coda 1   *D.S.S. al Coda 2*
(take repeat)

A7   E7   B7   B7   B7

4. Well, I   5. Yeah, I

Coda 2

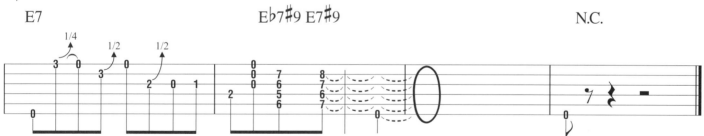

E7   E♭7♯9 E7♯9   N.C.

Additional Lyrics

2., 5. Yeah, I love my baby, my heart and soul.
Love like ours, uh, won't never grow old.
She's my sweet little thang, she's my pride and joy.
She's my sweet little baby, I'm her little lover boy.

4. Well, I love my baby like the finest wine.
Stick with her until the end of time. And she's my
Sweet little thang, she's my pride and joy.
She's my sweet little baby, I'm her little lover boy.

Love Struck Baby

Written by Stevie Ray Vaughan

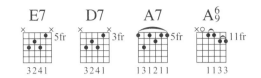

Key of A
Intro
Fast

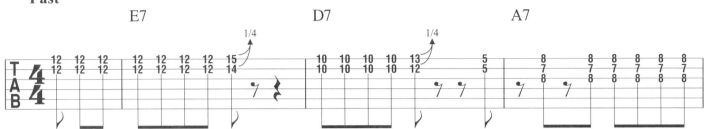

Chorus

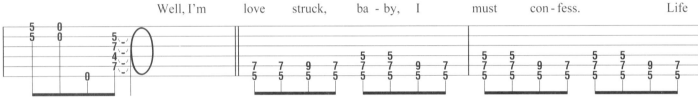

Well, I'm love struck, ba-by, I must con-fess. Life

etc.

with-out you, dar-lin', is a | sol-id mess. Think | -in' 'bout you, ba-by, give me

such a thrill. I got-ta | have you, ba-by, can't | get my fill. I

love you, ba-by, and I know just what to do.

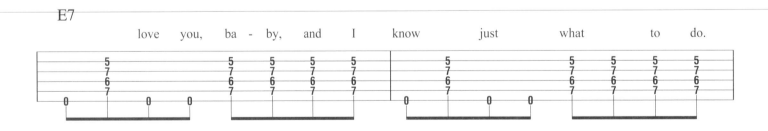

𝄋 **Verse**

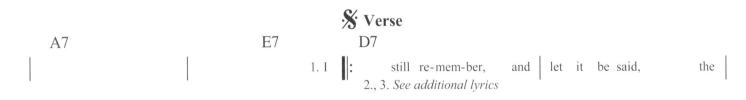

1. I 𝄆 still re-mem-ber, and | let it be said, the
2., 3. *See additional lyrics*

way you make me feel take a | fool to for-get. I | swore a ton o' bricks had hit me

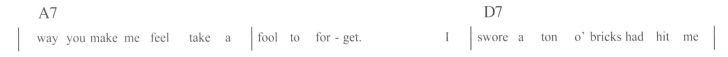

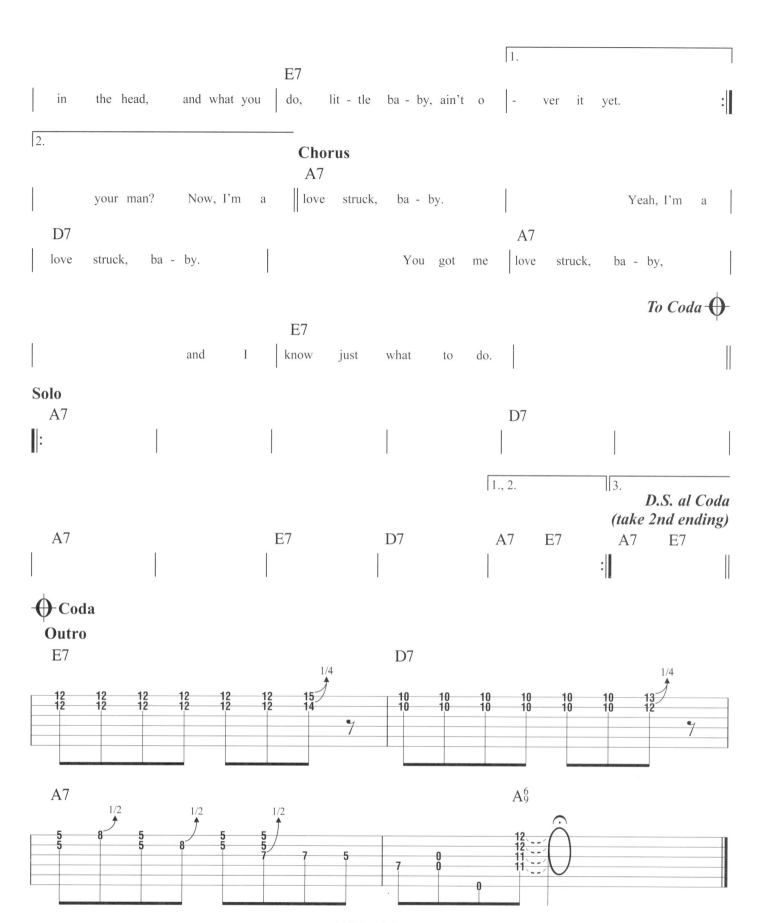

E7

| in the head, and what you | do, lit - tle ba - by, ain't o | - ver it yet. |

1.

2.

Chorus

A7

| your man? Now, I'm a ‖ love struck, ba - by. | Yeah, I'm a |

D7   **A7**

| love struck, ba - by. | You got me | love struck, ba - by, |

To Coda ⊕

E7

| and I | know just what to do. |

Solo

A7   **D7**

A7   **E7**   **D7**   **A7   E7**   **A7   E7**

1., 2.   *3.*

***D.S. al Coda
(take 2nd ending)***

⊕ **Coda**

Outro

E7   **D7**

A7   **A⁶₉**

Additional Lyrics

2. Everytime I see you, make me feel so fine.
   Heart beatin' crazy, my blood runnin' wild.
   Lovin' makes me feel like a mighty, mighty man.
   Love me, baby, ain't I your man?

3. Sparks start flyin' everytime we meet.
   Let me tell you, baby, you knock me off my feet.
   Your kisses trip me up and they're just dog gone sweet.
   Don't you know, baby, you can't be beat?

Man of Many Words

Words and Music by Buddy Guy

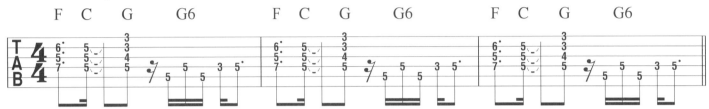

Key of G
Intro
    Moderately slow

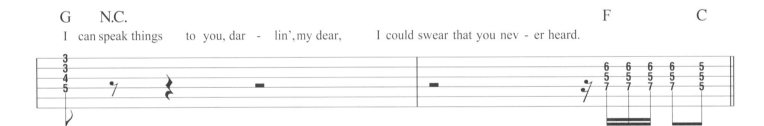

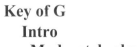**Verse**

1. I don't care what no-bod-y say, I'm a man of a man-y word,
2., 3. *See additional lyrics*

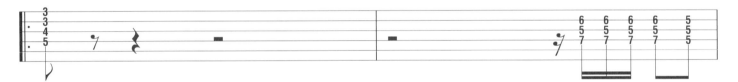

I can speak things to you, dar-lin', my dear, I could swear that you nev-er heard.

Chorus

To Coda ⊕

D9

I rap strong and I know I rap long, come on, ma-ma, let me turn you on, now come on.

N.C.

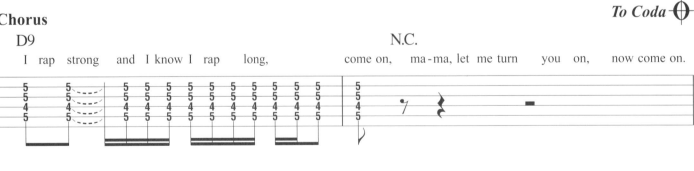

F   C   G   G6   F   C   G   G6

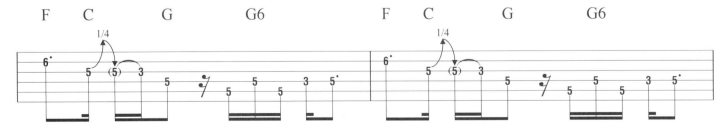

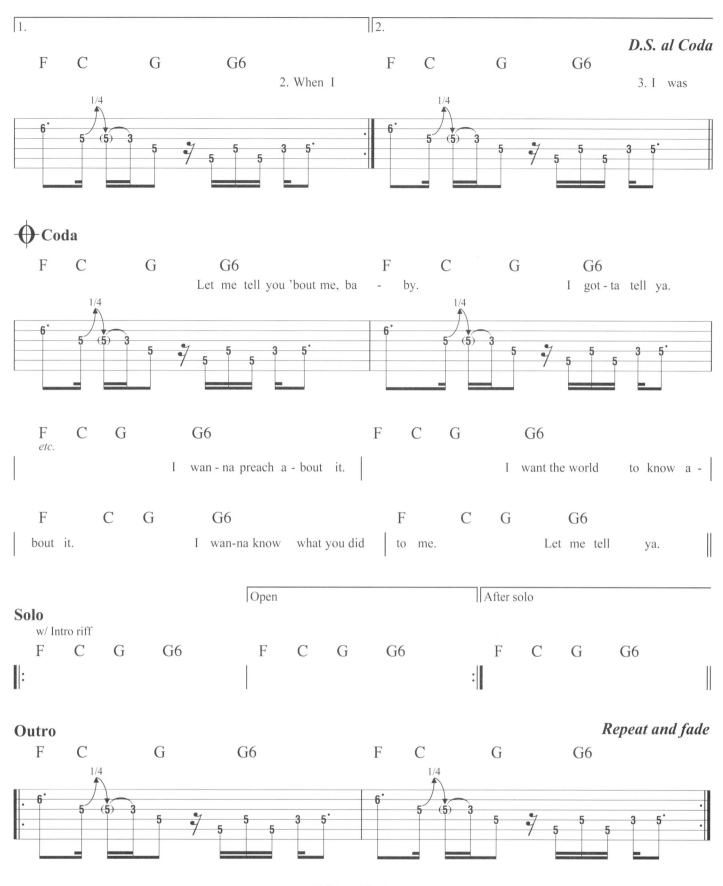

Additional Lyrics

2. When I rap my game and call your name,
   You will never be the same,
   In the midnight hours when you dream, my darlin',
   I swear you will call my name.

3. I was hauled off to jail late last night with
   No one to go my bail,
   I rapped strong to the judge early this morning
   And the judge put the cops in jail.

Mary Had a Little Lamb

Words and Music by Buddy Guy

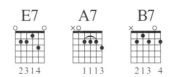

Key of E
Intro
Moderately

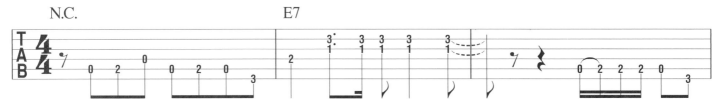

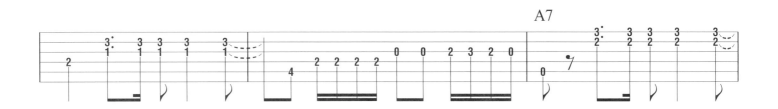

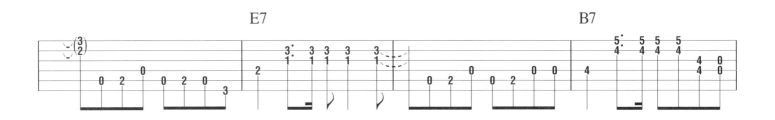

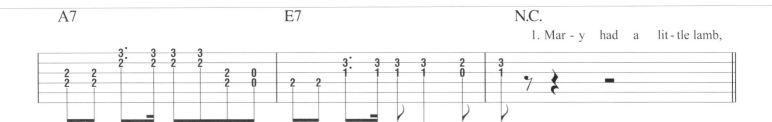

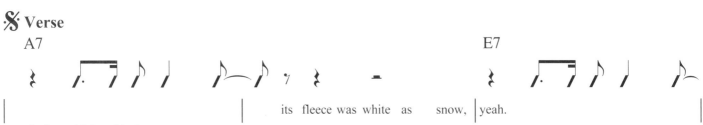

3. See additional lyrics
5. Instrumental

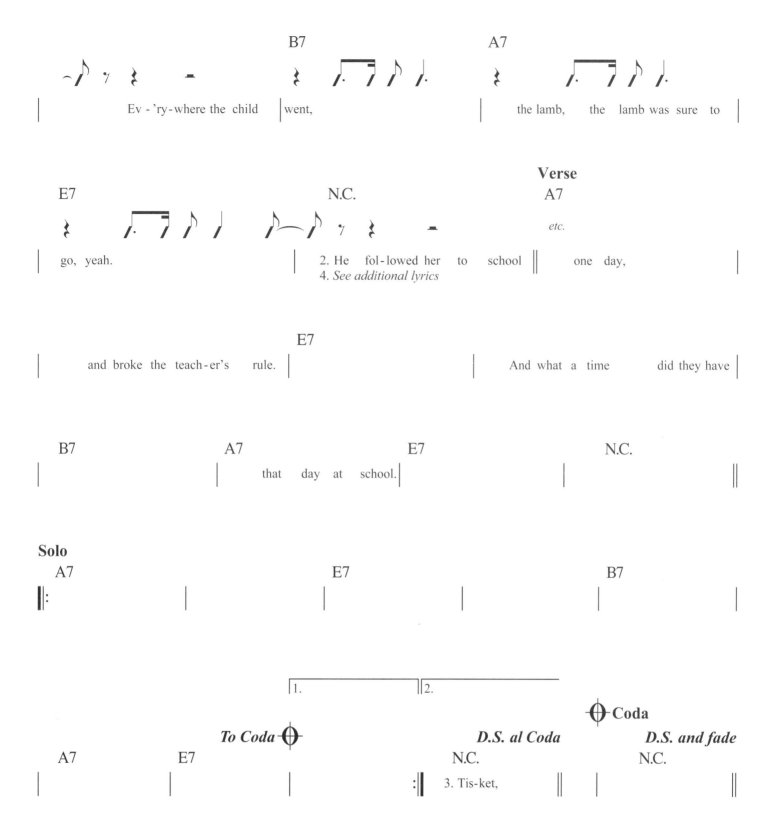

Ev - 'ry-where the child | went,   the lamb,   the lamb was sure to

go, yeah.   2. He fol-lowed her to school ‖ one day,
4. See additional lyrics

and broke the teach-er's rule.   And what a time did they have

that day at school.

Solo

To Coda ⊕

D.S. al Coda

D.S. and fade

⊕ **Coda**

3. Tis-ket,

Additional Lyrics

3. Tisket, tasket, baby, alright,
   A green and yellow basket, now.
   I wrote a letter to my baby,
   And on my way I passed it, now.

4. No, no, no, no, no, oo.
   No, no, no, no, yeah.
   No, no, no, no, no, yeah.
   No, no, no, no, no, no, yeah.

Messin' with the Kid

Words and Music by Mel London

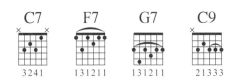

Key of C
Intro
Moderately fast

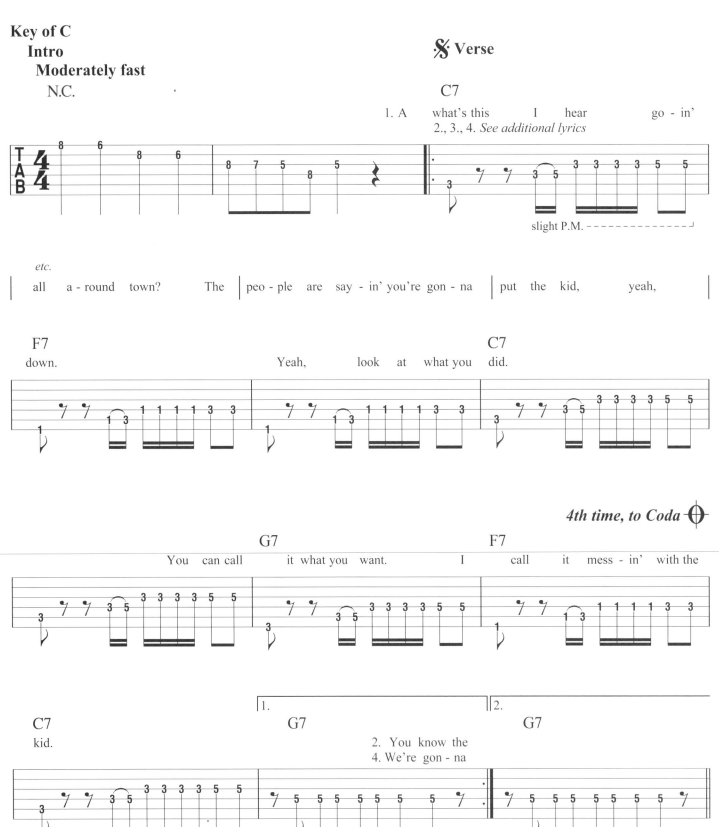

4th time, to Coda

Solo

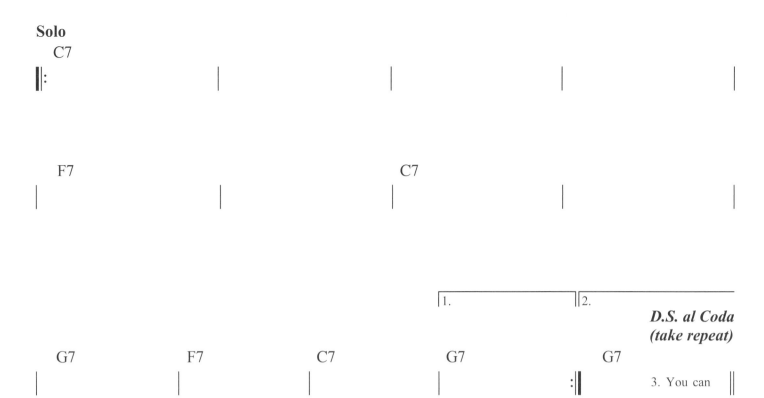

C7

F7   **C7**

1.   **2.**

D.S. al Coda
(take repeat)

G7   **F7**   **C7**   **G7**   **G7**

3. You can

Coda

Outro

N.C.   **C9**

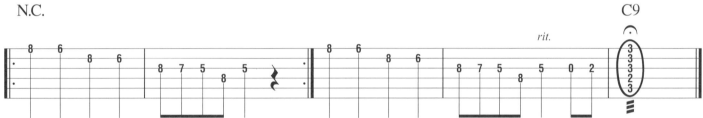

rit.

Additional Lyrics

2. You know the kid's no child and I don't play. I says what I mean. I mean what I say.
   But oh, yeah, yeah, yeah, yeah. Oh, look at what you did.
   You can call it what you want. I call it messin' with the kid.

3. You can tell me you love me. You tell me a lie. But I love you, baby, 'til the day I die.
   But oh, no. Oh, look at what you did.
   You can call it what you want. I call it messin' with the kid.

4. We're gonna take the kid's car and drive around town. And tell ev'rybody you're not puttin' him down.
   But oh, yeah, yeah, yeah, yeah. Oh, look at what you did.
   You can call it what you wanna. I call it messin' with the...

Mustang Sally

Words and Music by Bonny Rice

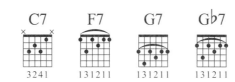

Key of C
Intro
Moderately
C7

1. Mus-tang   Sal -

Verse
C7
etc.

ly,   guess you bet - ter | slow your Mus - tang down.

Mus-tang

𝄋
F7

Sal - ly, now ba - by,   guess you bet - ter

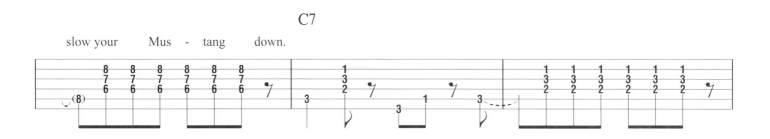

slow your   Mus - tang   down.   C7

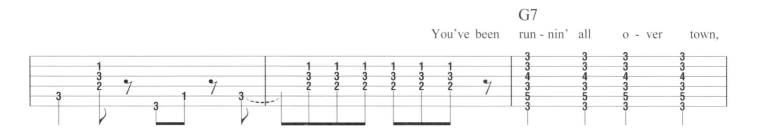

G7
You've been run - nin' all o - ver town,

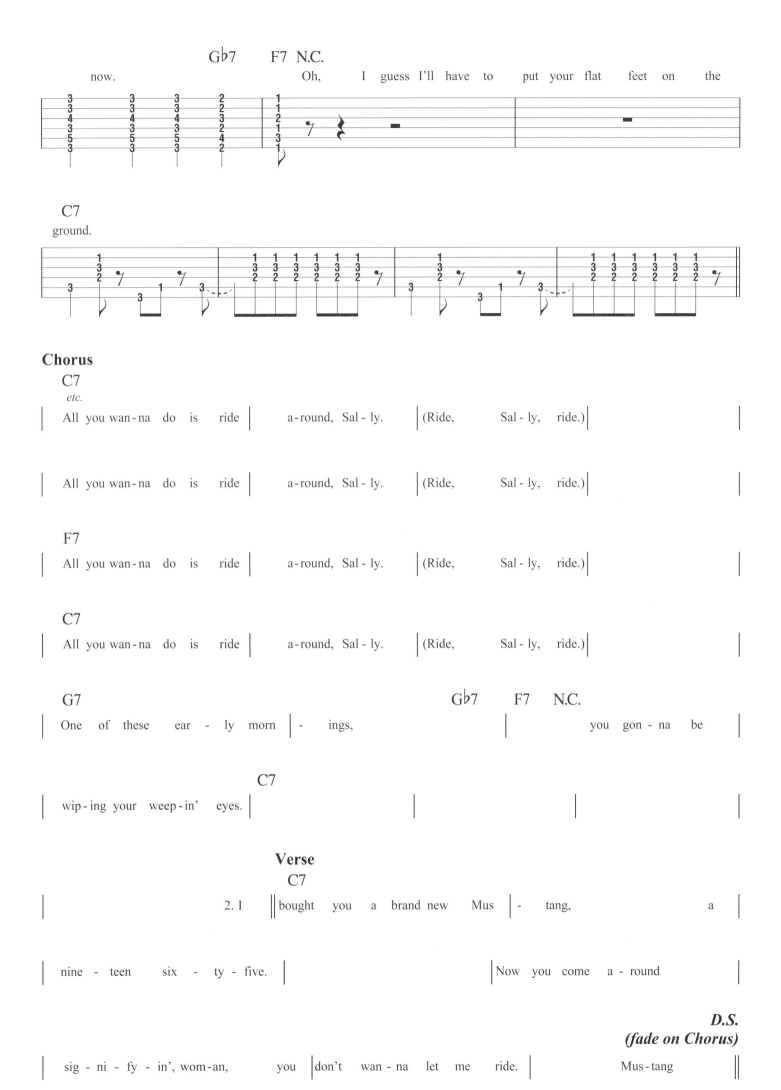

Chorus

C7
etc.

| All you wan-na do is ride | a-round, Sal-ly. | (Ride,   Sal-ly,   ride.) | |

| All you wan-na do is ride | a-round, Sal-ly. | (Ride,   Sal-ly,   ride.) | |

F7

| All you wan-na do is ride | a-round, Sal-ly. | (Ride,   Sal-ly,   ride.) | |

C7

| All you wan-na do is ride | a-round, Sal-ly. | (Ride,   Sal-ly,   ride.) | |

G7   G♭7   F7   N.C.

| One of these ear-ly morn | - ings, | you gon-na be | |

                       C7

| wip-ing your weep-in' eyes. | | | |

Verse

C7

| 2. I | bought you a brand new Mus | - tang, | a | |

| nine-teen six-ty-five. | | Now you come a-round | |

D.S.
(fade on Chorus)

| sig-ni-fy-in', wom-an, you | don't wan-na let me ride. | Mus-tang | ‖ |

Reconsider Baby

Words and Music by Lowell Fulson

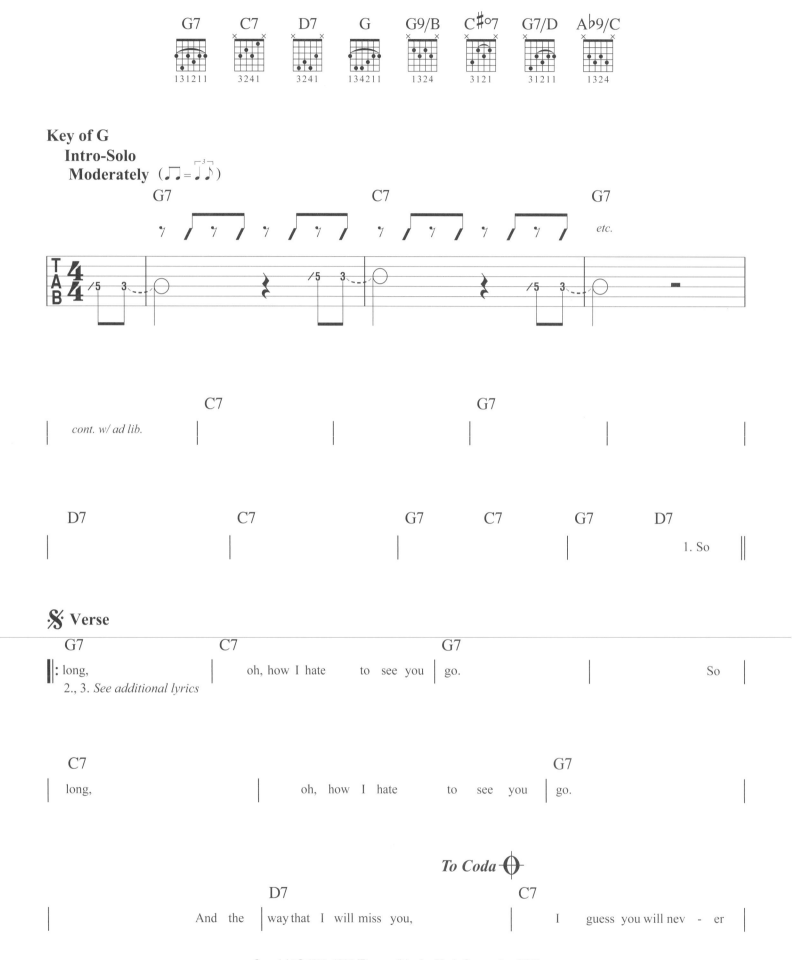

Key of G
Intro-Solo
Moderately

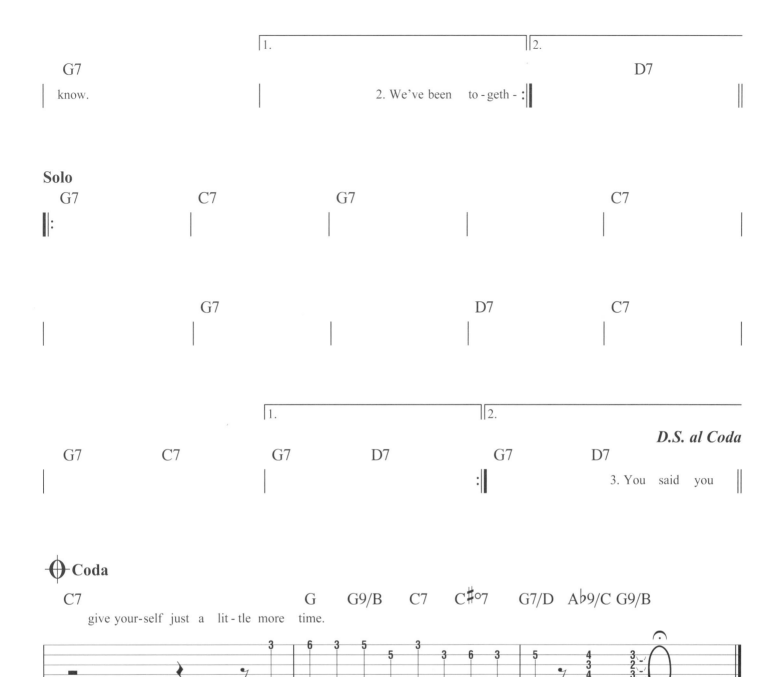

Additional Lyrics

2. We've been together so long to have to separate this way.
   We've been together so long to have to separate this way.
   I'm gonna let you go ahead on, baby, pray that you'll come back home some day.

3. You said you once had loved me, but now I guess you have changed your mind.
   You said you once had loved me, but now I guess you have changed your mind.
   Why don't you reconsider, baby, give yourself just a little more time.

Red House

Words and Music by Jimi Hendrix

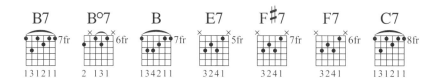

Key of B
Intro
Moderately slow

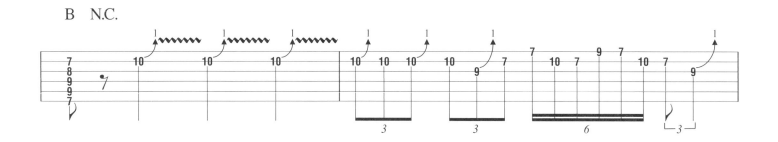

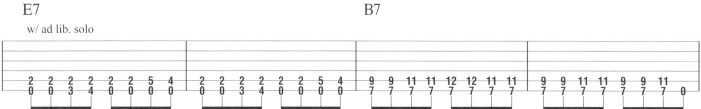

Verse

B7

etc.

E7

red house   o - ver yon - der,   that's where my   ba - by   stays.

2., 4. *See additional lyrics*

3. *Instrumental*

B7   E7

Lord, there's a red house   o-ver yon-der,

                              B7

Lord, that's where   my ba-by stays.

4th time, to Coda ⊕

F#7   E7

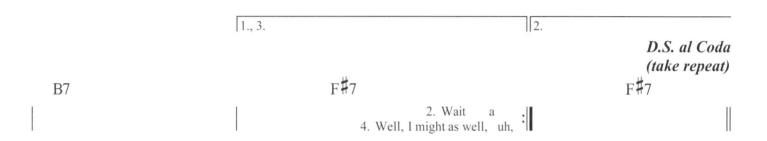

I ain't been home to see my   ba-by   in nine-ty-nine and one-half days.

1., 3.	2.

D.S. al Coda
(take repeat)

B7   F#7   F#7

2. Wait   a
4. Well, I might as well, uh,

⊕ **Coda**

E7 N.C.   B7   E7   F#7   C7 B7

I know her   sis-ter will.

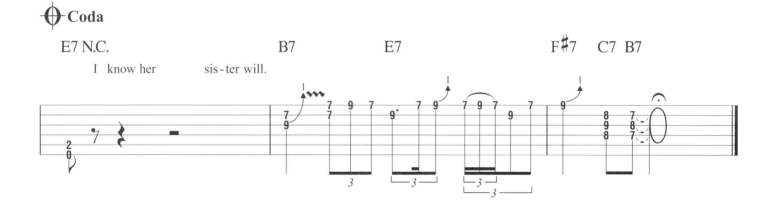

Additional Lyrics

2. Wait a minute, something's wrong here; this key won't unlock this door.
   Wait a minute, something's wrong; Lord, have mercy, this key won't unlock this door.
   I have a bad, bad feelin', uh, that my baby don't live here no more.

4. Well, I might as well, uh, go back over yonder, way back among the hills.
   Lord, I might as well go back over yonder, way back yonder 'cross the hill.
   'Cause if my baby don't love me no more, I know her sister will.

Rock Me Baby

Words and Music by B.B. King and Joe Bihari

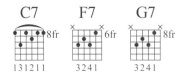

Key of C
Intro
Moderately slow

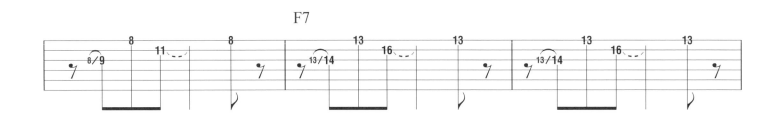

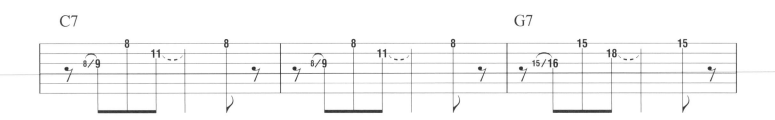

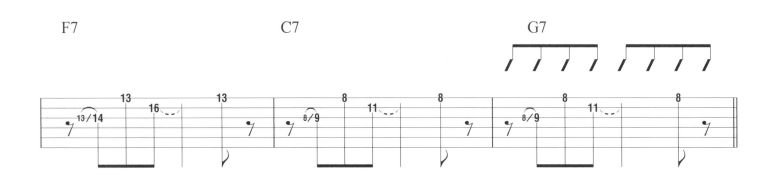

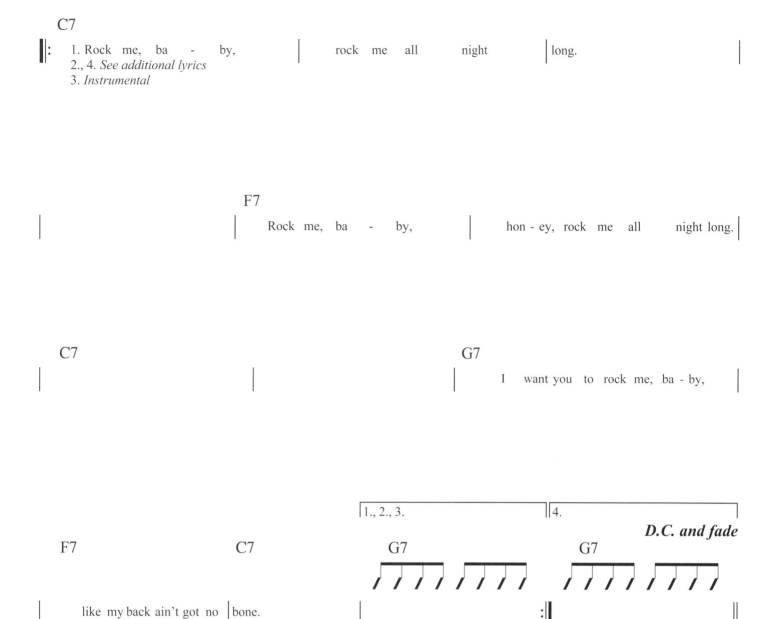

C7

$\lVert$: 1. Rock me, ba - by, | rock me all night | long. |
2., 4. *See additional lyrics*
3. *Instrumental*

F7

| Rock me, ba - by, | hon - ey, rock me all night long. |

C7   G7

| | | I want you to rock me, ba - by, |

1., 2., 3.   4.

D.C. and fade

F7   C7   G7   G7

| like my back ain't got no | bone. | :$\lVert$ | $\lVert$

Additional Lyrics

2. Roll me, baby, like you roll a wagon wheel.
   Want you to roll me, baby, like you roll a wagon wheel.
   Want you to roll me, baby, you don't know how it makes me feel.

4. Rock me, baby, honey, rock me slow.
   Hey, rock me, pretty baby. Baby, rock me slow.
   Want you to rock me, baby, 'til I want no more.

Satisfy Susie

Words and Music by Lonnie McIntosh and Tim Drummond

Key of E
   Intro
   Moderately

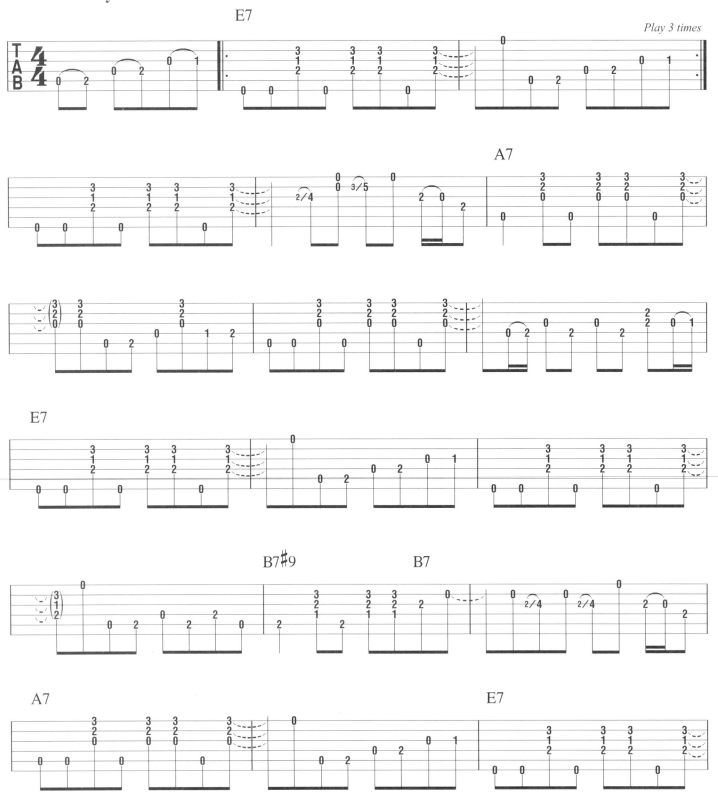

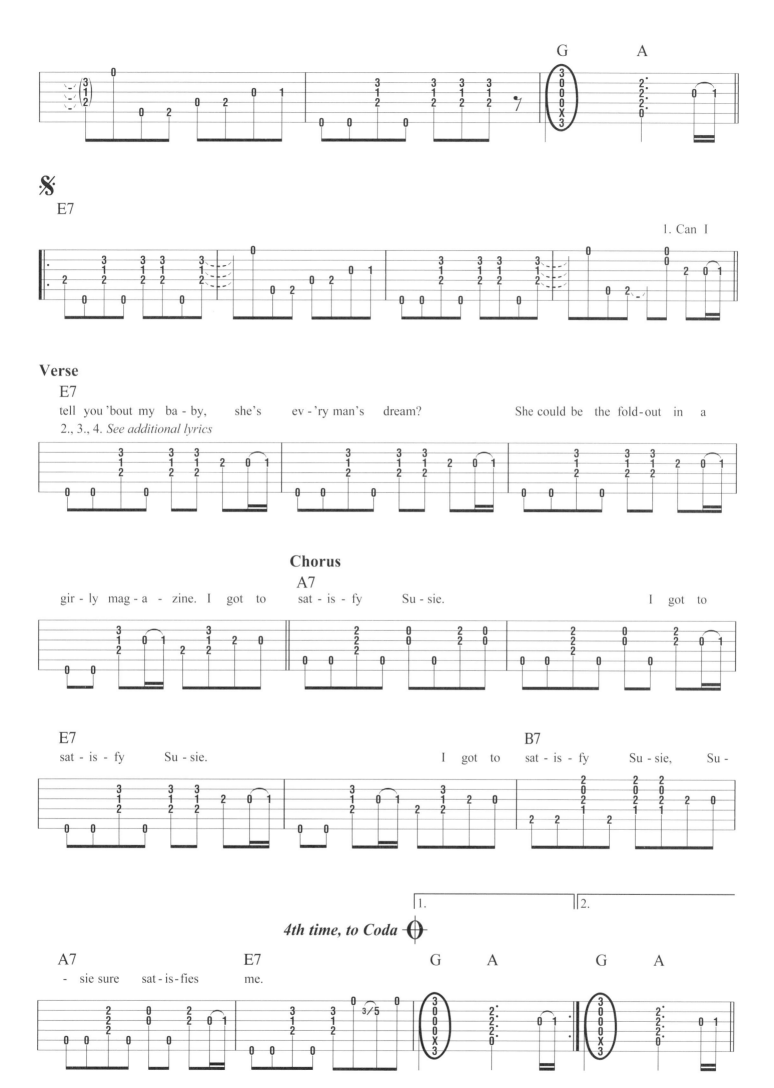

Solo

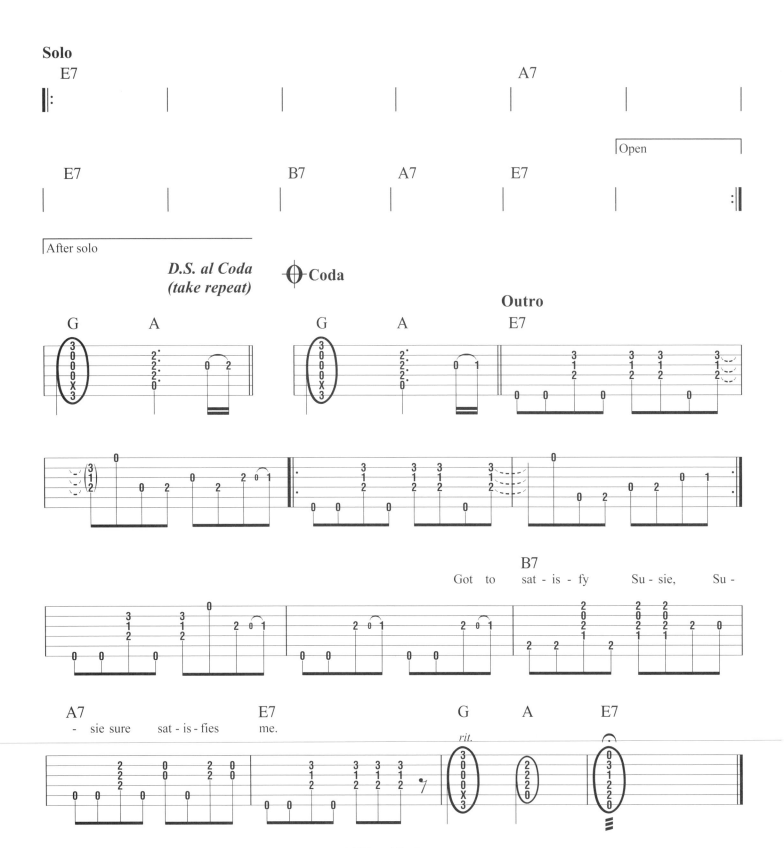

Got to sat - is - fy Su - sie, Su - sie sure sat - is - fies me.

rit.

Additional Lyrics

2. Bought a brand new Chevy,
   Keep it shined up in the drive.
   Souped up to the limit
   'Cause Susie likes to fly.

3. Susie's into lovin'
   Anyway you can.
   She don't give her lovin'
   To any other man.

4. You ask me if I'm happy,
   Do I look satisfied?
   Susie's got the way to keep
   The twinkle in my eye.

Smokestack Lightning

Words and Music by Chester Burnett

Verse

w/ Intro riff throughout

E7

1. Oh,   oh,   smoke - stack   light - nin',   shin - in'
2.-6. *See additional lyrics*

          just   like   gold.   Oh,   don't   you   hear   me   cry - ing?

Woo-ohh.   Woo-ooh.

Woo - ooh.

1.-5. | 6.

Repeat and fade

Outro

E7

Additional Lyrics

2. Oh, oh, tell me, baby, what's the matter here?
   Oh, don't you hear me crying? Woo-ooh. Woo-ooh. Woo-ooh.

3. Whoa, oh, tell me, baby, where did you stay last night?
   Oh, don't you hear me crying? Woo-ooh. Woo-ooh. Woo-ooh.

4. Whoa, oh, stop your train, let a poor boy ride.
   Whoa, don't you hear me crying? Woo-ooh. Woo-ooh. Woo-ooh.

5. Whoa, oh, fare you well, never see you no more.
   Oh, don't you hear me crying? Woo-ooh. Woo-ooh. Woo-ooh.

6. Oh, oh, who been here, baby, since I been gone?
   Little bitty boy? Girl, be on. Woo-ooh. Woo-ooh. Woo-ooh.

Shake for Me

Written by Willie Dixon

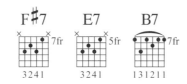

Key of B
Intro
Moderately

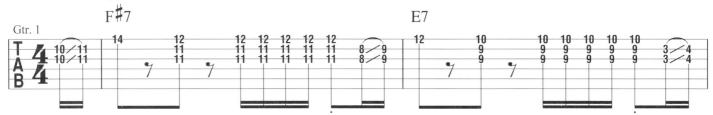

*Strum muted strings

1. Sure

𝄋 Verse

Gtr. 1: *etc.*

B7

look good, but you don't mean a thing to me.
2., 4., 5. *See additional lyrics*
3., 6. *Instrumental*

Gtr. 2

E7

Sure look good, but you don't mean a thing

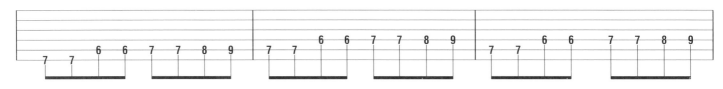

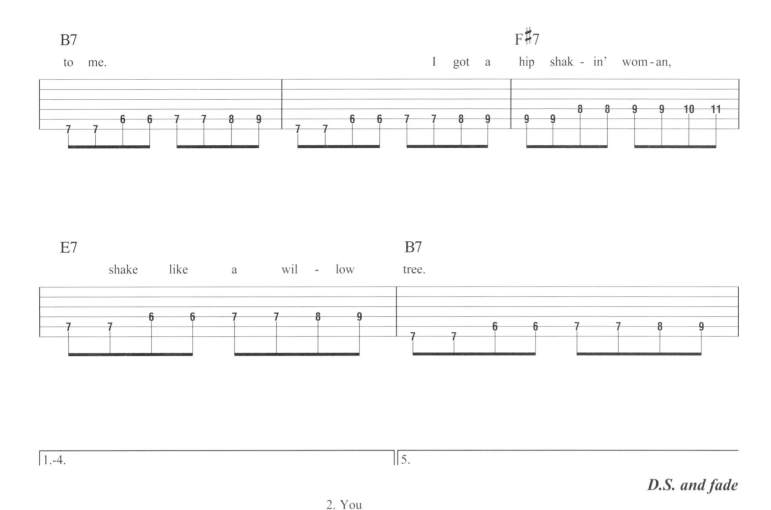

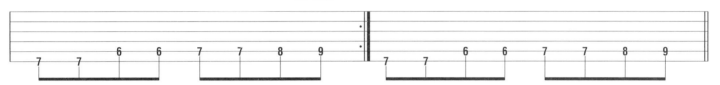

Additional Lyrics

2. You went away, baby, you got back a little too late.
   You went away, baby, you got back a little too late.
   I got a cool shakin' baby, shake like Jell-o on a plate.

4. When my baby walk, you know she's fine and mellow.
   When my baby walk, you know she's fine and mellow.
   Every time she stop, her flesh, it shake like Jell-o.

5. Oh, shake it, baby, shake it for me.
   Oh, shake, little baby, shake it for me.
   Oh, shake it, little baby, just shake like a willow tree.

She's Into Somethin'

Words and Music by Carl Wright

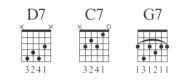

D7   C7   G7

Key of G
Intro
Moderate Rhumba

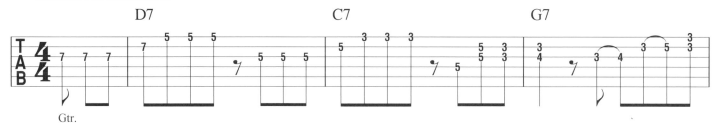

Gtr.

𝄋 **Verse**

N.C.   G7

Shouted: Say what she do!   1. The   snap-pin' of her fin-ger makes a   dog   wag his tail,
2., 3. *See additional lyrics*

Bass arr. for gtr.

etc.
    the whis-tle from her voice   make a | train   jump the rail.   Take her to a   race-track,

N.C.

    show her face,   horse | that ain't won in years comes in | first   place.   You know that ‖

Chorus

C7   G7
    she's   in-to   some-thing, | yeah, | she's   in-to   some-thing.

To Coda ⊕

    D7   C7
    She's   in-to   some-thing, | you   should be   in-to   some-

1.	2.
G7 D7	G7 D7
thing, too.	2. Well, you :‖ thing, too.	

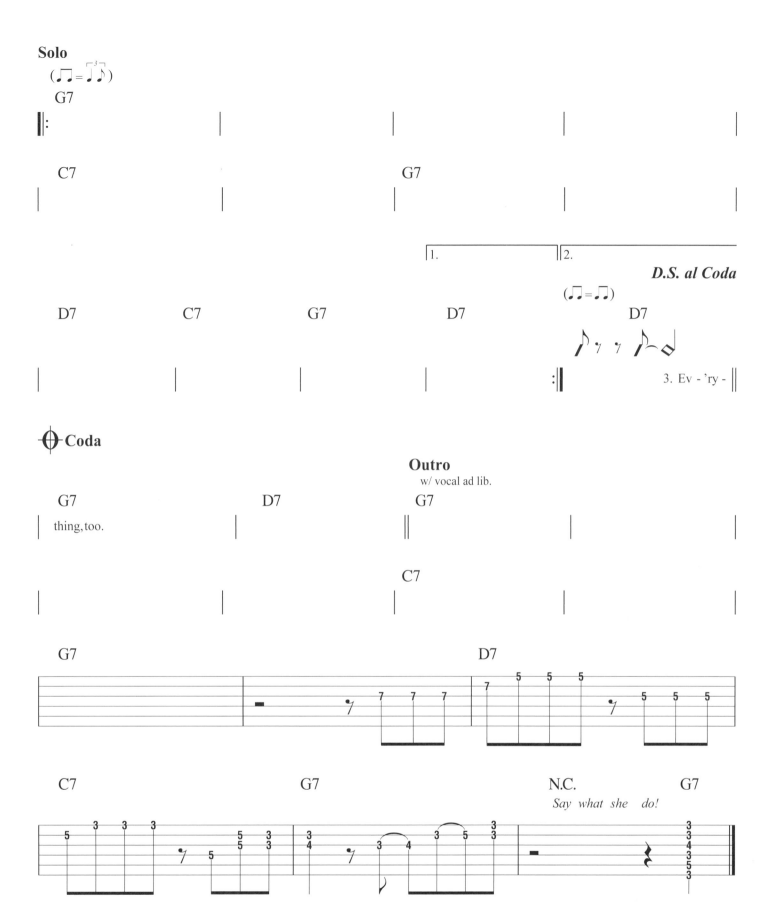

Additional Lyrics

2. Well, you laughed at her about a week ago,
   Now she's met a man with a whole lot of dough.
   And, oh, yeah, he's rich, I've seen the money.
   All she had to do was call the man honey, honey, honey.

3. Ev'ryday of her life she rides around on wheels,
   And, oh, yeah, you might say she's got herself a stone cold deal.
   One thing the girl, she don't have to do is
   Worry about no money when the payment's due.

Smoking Gun

Words and Music by Bruce Bromberg, Richard Cousins and Robert Cray

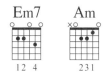

Key of Em
Intro
Moderately

Em7

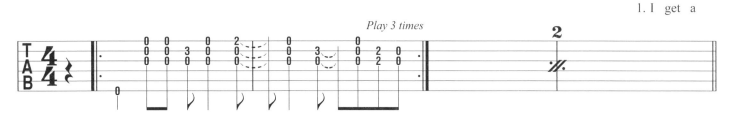

1. I get a

%Verse

w/ Intro pattern

Em7

con - stant bus - y sig - |nal   when I | call you on   the phone. | I get a |
2., 5. *See additional lyrics*
3., 4. *Instrumental*

strong un - ea - sy feel |- ing   you're not | sit - ting there a - lone. | I'm hav - ing |

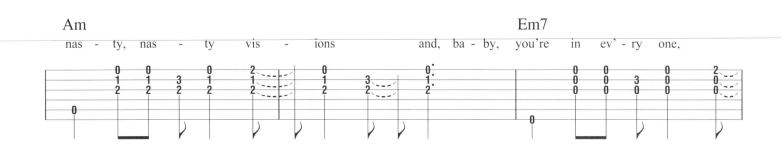

nas - ty, nas - ty vis - ions   and, ba - by, you're in ev' - ry one,

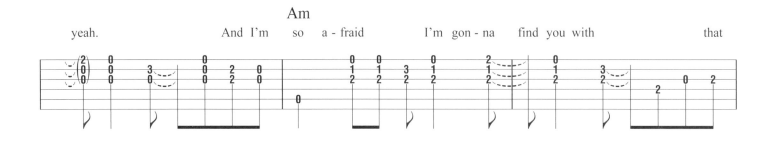

yeah.   And I'm so a - fraid   I'm gon - na find you with   that

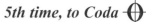
N.C.   Em7

so call - ed smok - in' gun.

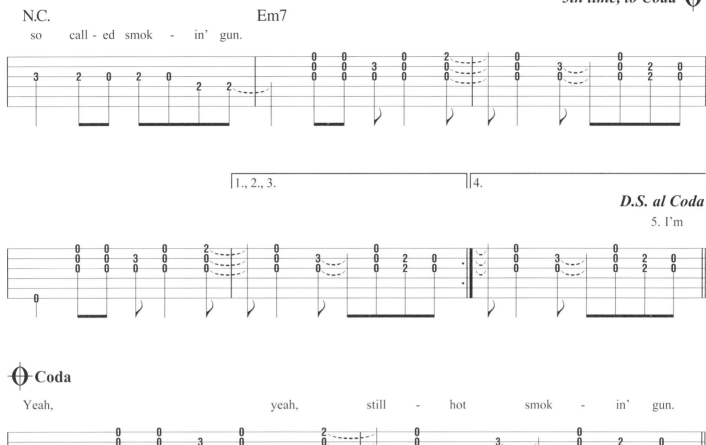

Coda

Yeah,   yeah, still - hot smok - in' gun.

Outro

w/ vocal & guitar ad lib.

Repeat and fade

Em7

etc.

They've | tak - en it; | still - hot smok - in' gun.

Additional Lyrics

2. Maybe you wanna end it;
 You've had your fill of my kind of fun.
 But you don't know how to tell me,
 And you know that I'm not that dumb.
 I put two and one together,
 And we know that's not an even sum.
 And I know just where to catch you with
 That well-known smoking gun.

5. I'm standing here bewildered;
 I can't remember just what I've done.
 I can hear the sirens whining,
 My eyes blinded by the sun.
 I know that I should be running;
 My heart's beating just like a drum.
 Now they've knocked me down and taken it,
 That still-hot smoking gun.

Someone Else Is Steppin' In

Words and Music by Dennis LaSalle

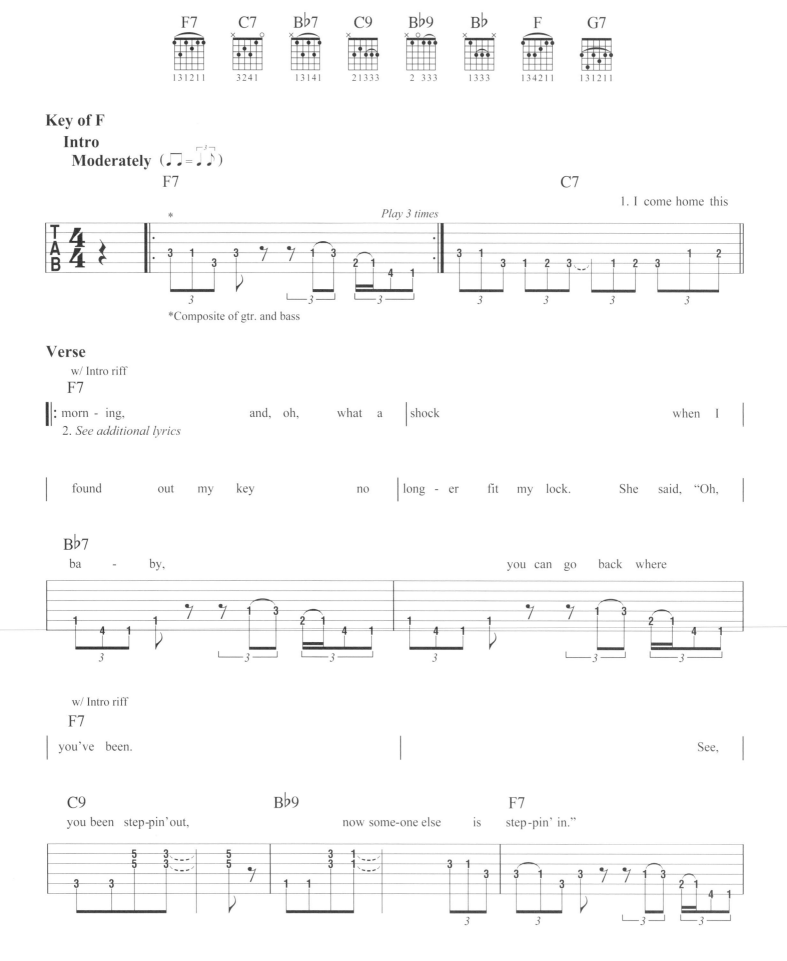

Key of F

Intro

Moderately

Composite of gtr. and bass

Verse

w/ Intro riff

F7

morn - ing,   and, oh,   what a | shock   when I |

2. See additional lyrics

found   out my key   no | long - er fit my lock.   She said, "Oh,

Bb7

ba - by,   you can go back where

w/ Intro riff

F7

you've been.   See,

C9   Bb9   F7

you been step-pin'out,   now some-one else is step-pin' in."

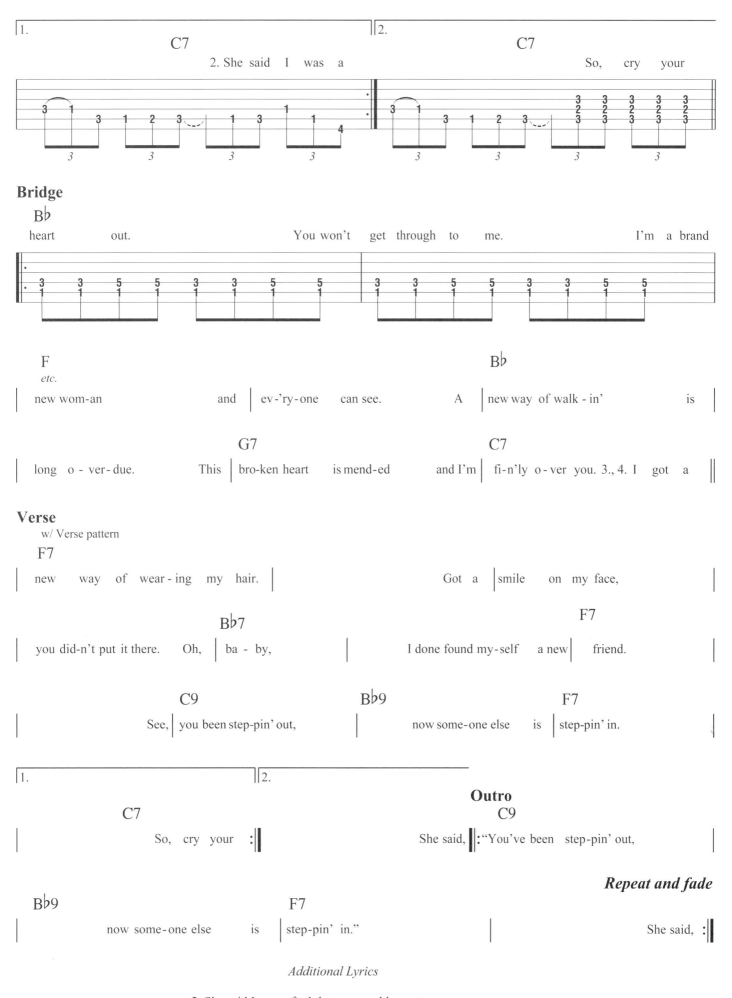

Bridge

Verse
w/ Verse pattern

Outro

Repeat and fade

Additional Lyrics

2. She said I was a fool that you could count on.
   The one that you could call when no one else was at home.
   Oh, baby, remember how you treated me then.
   See, you've been steppin' out, now someone else is steppin' in.

Still Got the Blues

Words and Music by Gary Moore

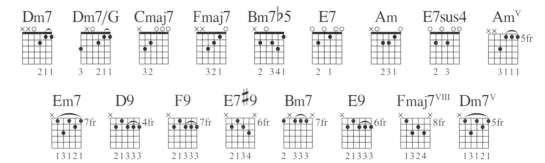

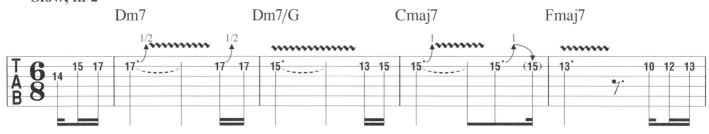

Key of Am
Intro
Slow, in 2

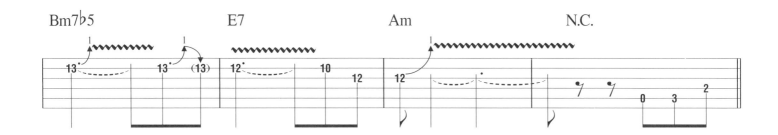

𝄌 Verse

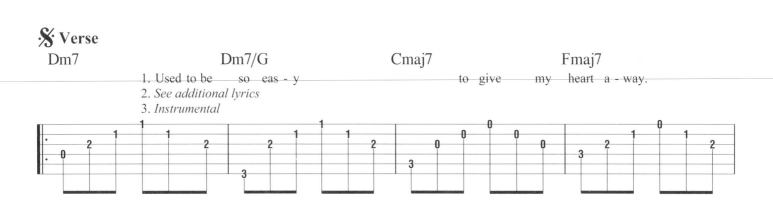

1. Used to be so eas-y to give my heart a-way.
2. *See additional lyrics*
3. *Instrumental*

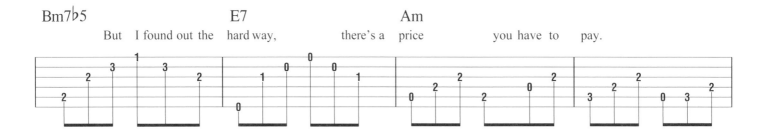

But I found out the hard way, there's a price you have to pay.

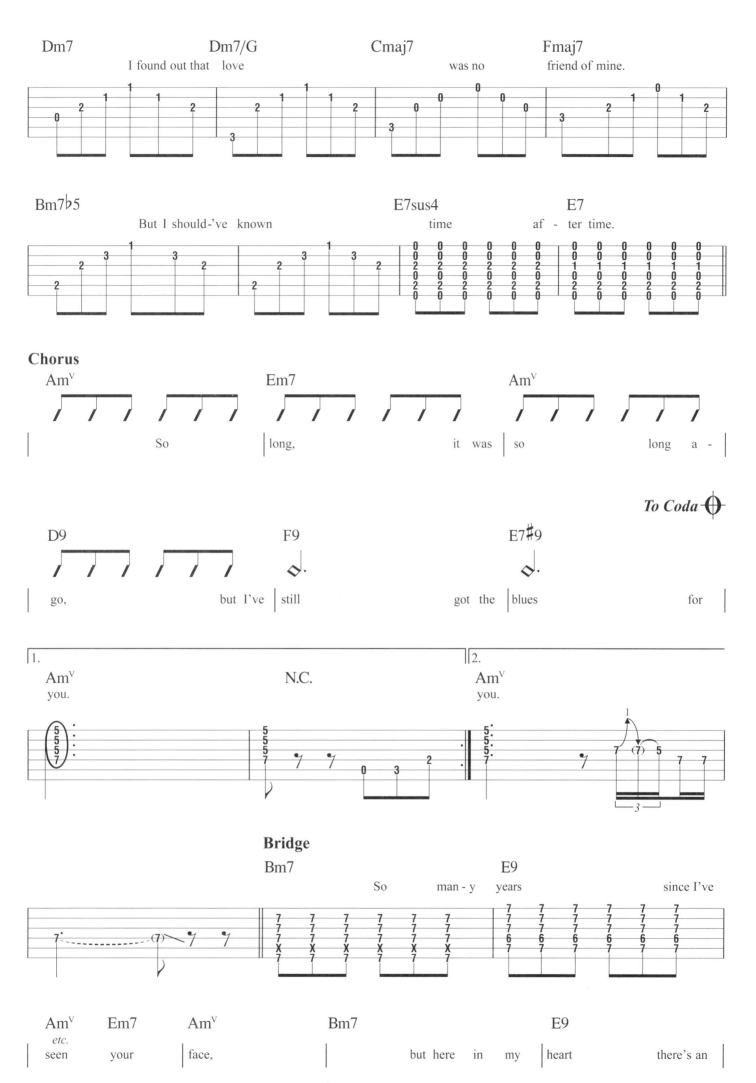

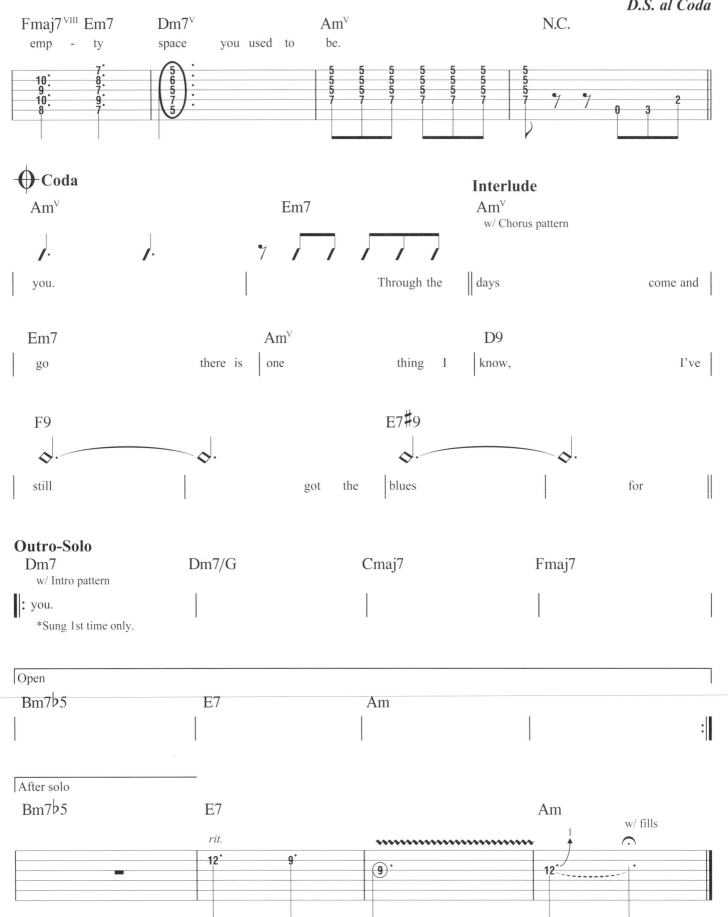

Outro-Solo

*Sung 1st time only.

Additional Lyrics

2. Used to be so easy to fall in love again.
But I found out the hard way, it's a road that leads to pain.
But I found out that love was more than just a game.
You're playin' to win, but you'll lose just the same.

Wham

By Lonnie Mack

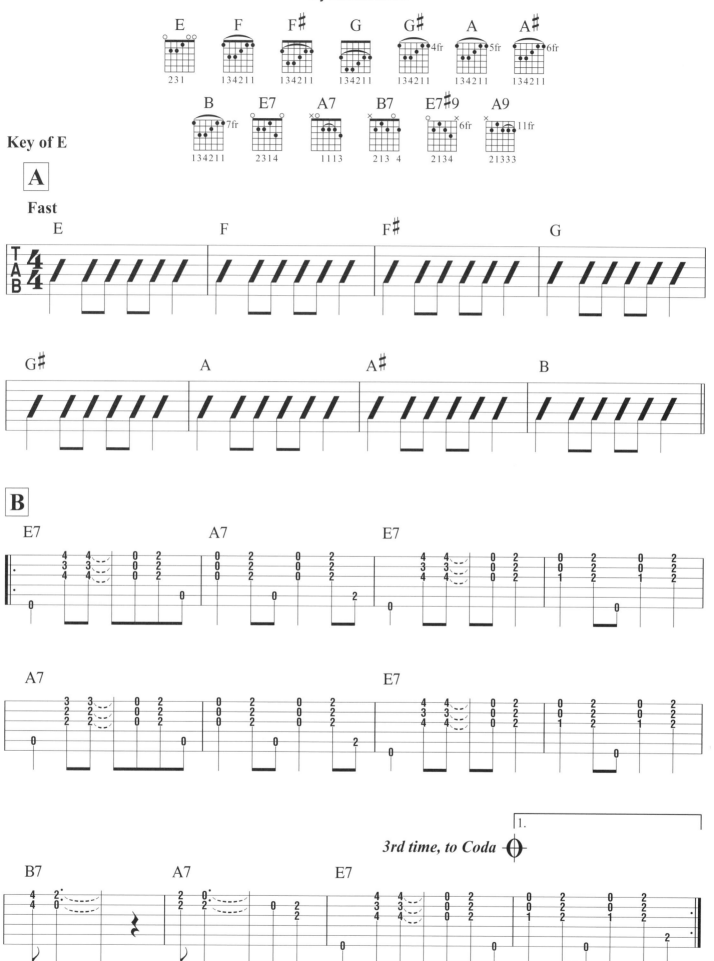

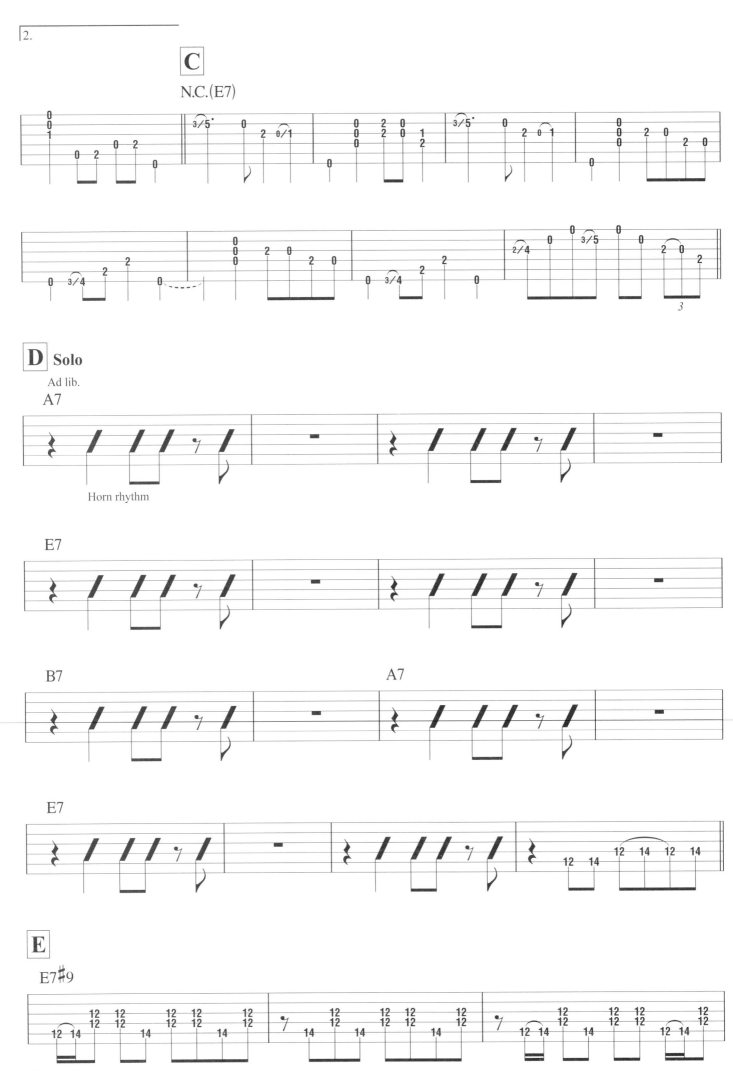

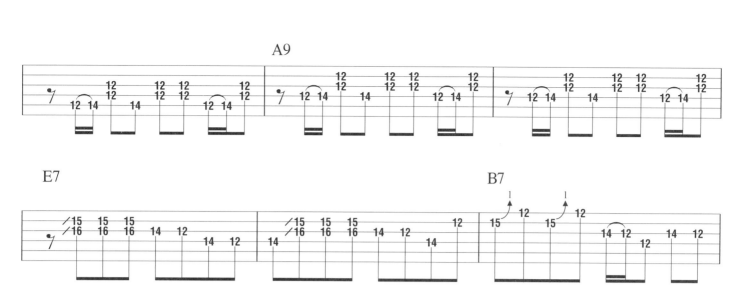

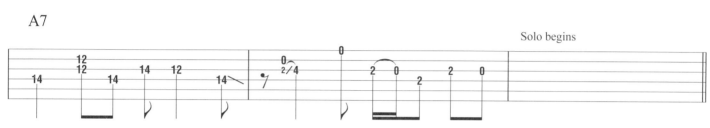

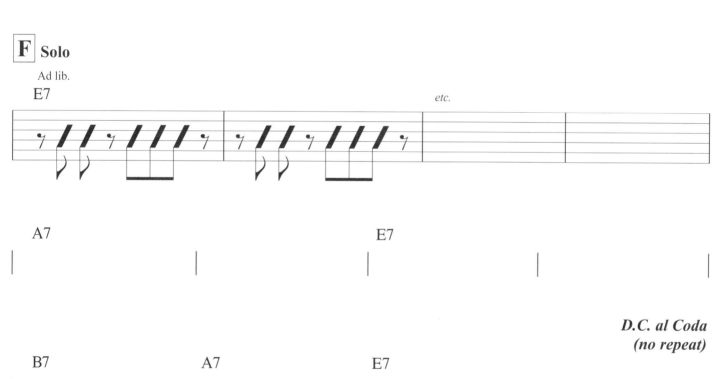

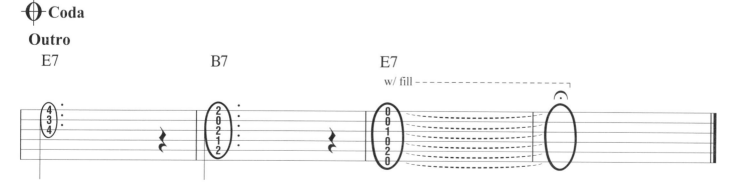

T-Bone Shuffle

By T-Bone Walker

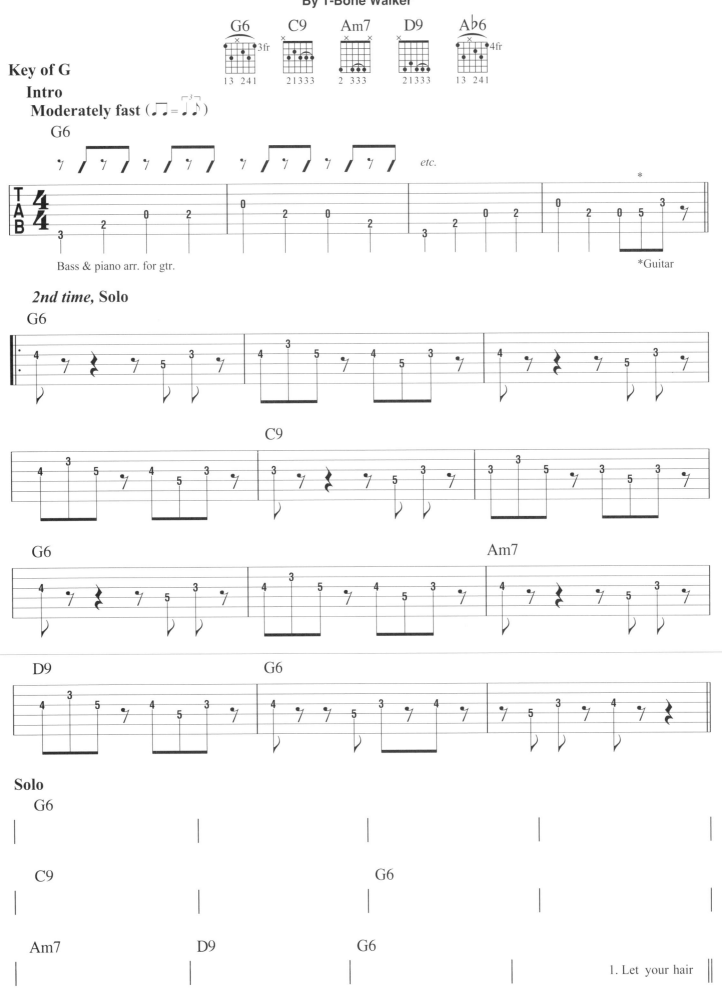

𝄋 Verse

G6

| down ba - by, and let's have | a nat -'ral ball. | | | Let your hair |

2., 3. *See additional lyrics*

C9   G6

| down, ba - by, and let's have | a nat -'ral ball. | | 'Cause when |

To Coda ⊕   1.

Am7   D9   G6

| you're not hap - py, | it ain't no fun at all. | | :‖ |

2.

Solo
G6

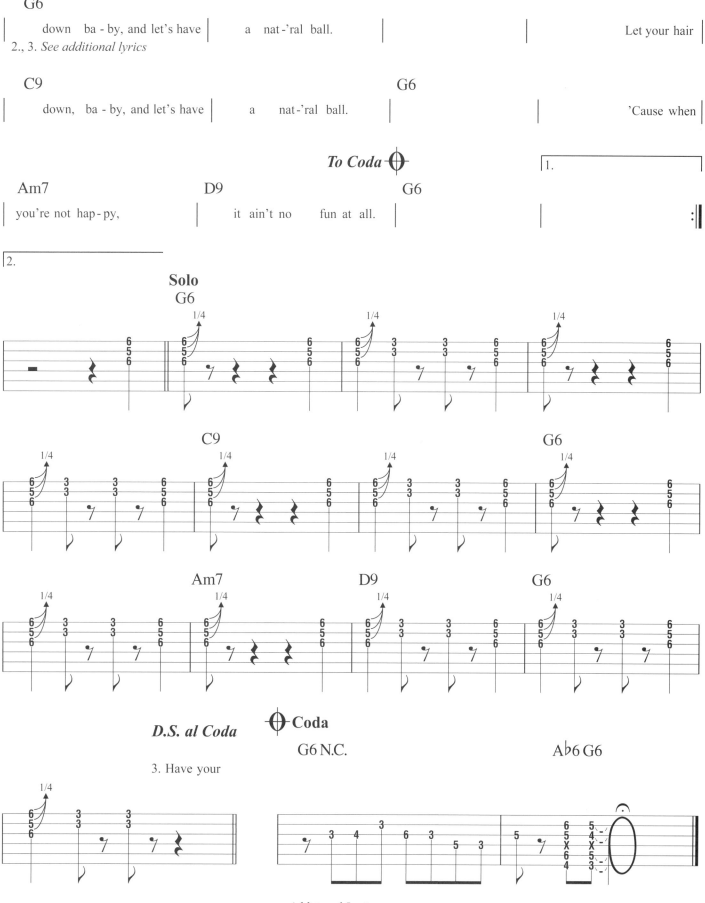

C9   G6

Am7   D9   G6

D.S. al Coda   ⊕ **Coda**

G6 N.C.   A♭6 G6

3. Have your

Additional Lyrics

2. You can't take it with you, that's one thing for sure.
You can't take it with you, that's one thing for sure.
There's nothing wrong with you that a good shuffle boogie won't cure.

3. Have your fun while you can, fate's an awful thing.
Have your fun while you can, fate's an awful thing.
You can't tell what might happen, that's why I love to sing.

The Thrill Is Gone

Words and Music by Roy Hawkins and Rick Darnell

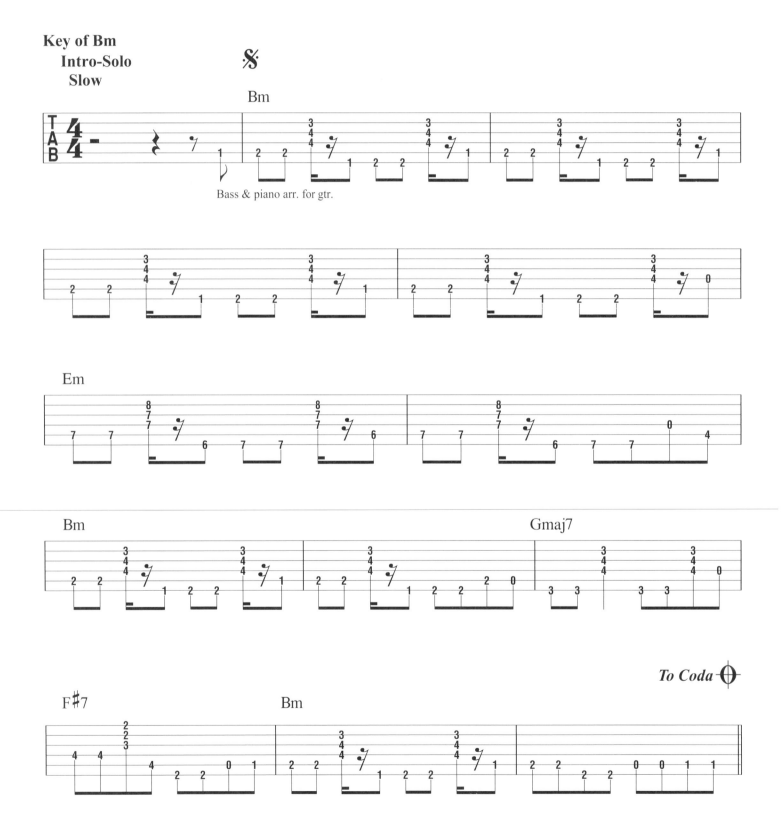

Verse

Bm

etc.

‖: 1. The thrill is gone,   the thrill is gone | a - way. |
2., 4., 5. *See additional lyrics*
3. *Instrumental*

Em

| The thrill is gone,   ba - by, | the thrill is gone |

Bm   **Gmaj7**

| a - way. | | You know you done me wrong,   ba - |

| 1.-4. | 5. |

D.S. al Coda

F♯7   **Bm**

| - by,   and you'll be sor | - ry some - day. | :‖ ‖

⊕ **Coda**

Repeat and fade

Outro-Solo

Bm

‖: | | | :‖

Additional Lyrics

2. The thrill is gone, it's gone away from me.
   The thrill is gone, baby, the thrill is gone away from me.
   Although I'll still live on,
   But so lonely I'll be.

4. The thrill is gone, it's gone away for good.
   Oh, the thrill is gone, baby, it's gone away for good.
   Someday I know I'll be over it all, baby,
   Just like I know a good man should.

5. You know I'm free, free now, baby, I'm free from your spell.
   Whoa, I'm free, free, free now, I'm free from your spell.
   And now that it's all over,
   All I can do is wish you well.

Tuff Enuff
Words and Music by Kim Wilson

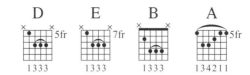

Key of B
Intro
Moderately

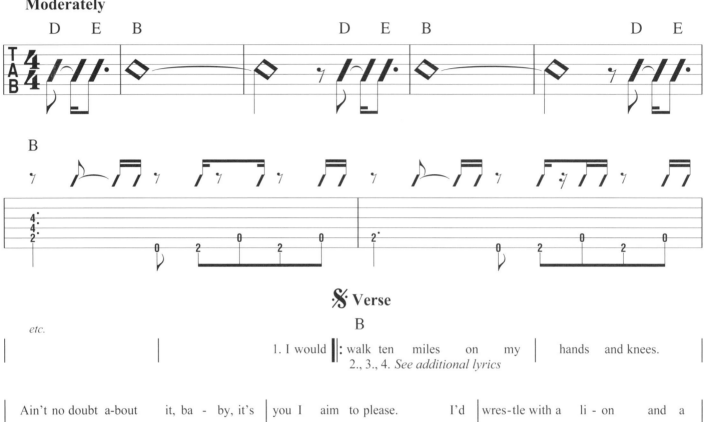

𝄋 Verse

etc.

1. I would ‖: walk ten miles on my | hands and knees.
2., 3., 4. *See additional lyrics*

Ain't no doubt a-bout it, ba - by, it's | you I aim to please. I'd | wres-tle with a li - on and a

4th time, to Coda 1 ⊕

| griz - zly bear. It's | my life, ba - by, but | I don't care. Ain't that ‖

𝄋𝄋 Chorus

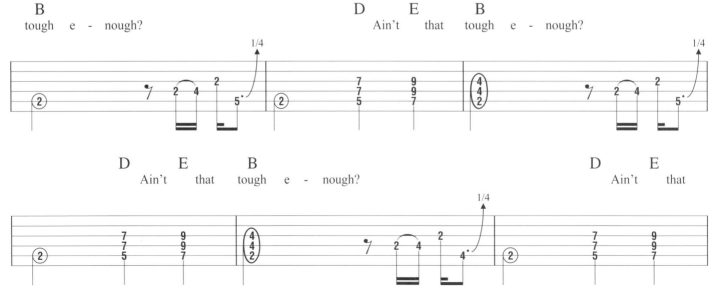

B
tough e - nough?

D E B
Ain't that tough e - nough?

D E B
Ain't that tough e - nough?

D E
Ain't that

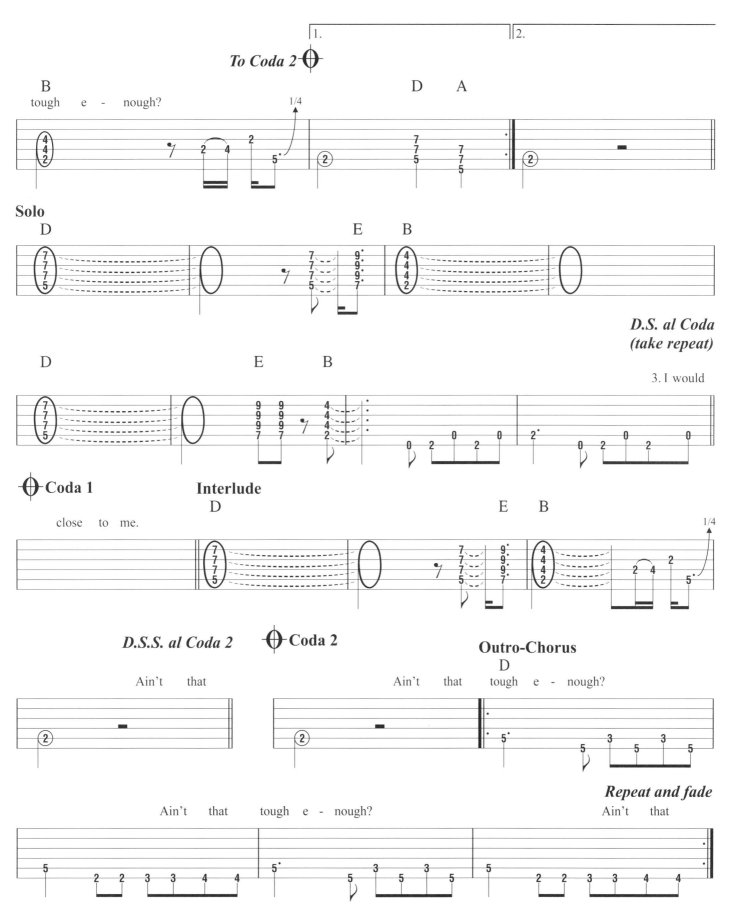

Additional Lyrics

2. For you, baby, I would swim the sea.
   Nothin' I'd do for you that's too tough for me.
   I'd put out a burnin' buildin' with a shovel and dirt
   And not even worry about getting hurt.

3. I would work twenty-four hours, seven days a week
   Just so I can come home and kiss your cheek.
   I'll love you in the mornin' and I'll love you at noon.
   I'll love you in the night and take you to the moon.

4. I'd lay in a pile of burnin' money that I've earned
   And not even worry about getting burned.
   I'd climb the Empire State, fight Muhammad Ali
   Just to have you, baby, close to me.

Wang Dang Doodle

Words and Music by Willie Dixon

F7#9

Key of F
Intro
Moderately, in 2

F7#9

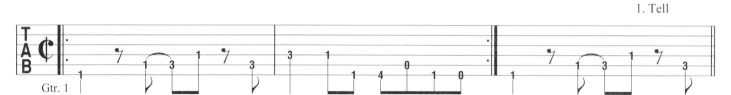

§ **Verse**

Gtr. 1: w/ Intro riff throughout

F7#9

Au - to - mat - ic Slim,   tell Ra - zor To - tin' Jim.   Tell
2., 3. *See additional lyrics*

Butch - er Knife To - tin' An - nie,   tell Fast Talk - in' Fan -

nie.   We gon - na pitch a ball,   a down

*V = upstroke

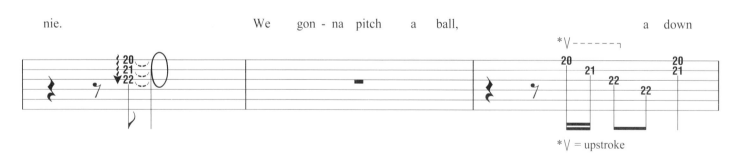

etc.
to that un - ion hall.   We gon - na romp and tromp 'til mid -

- night, we gon - na fuss and fight 'til day - light. We gon - na

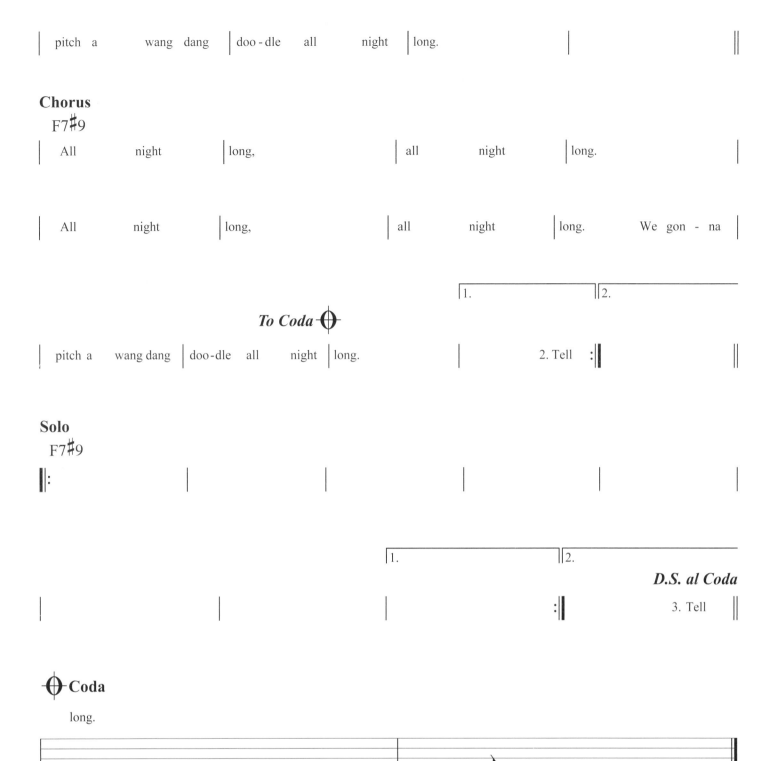

Additional Lyrics

2. Tell 'Cuda Crawlin' Red, tell Abyssinian Ned.
   Go tell old Pistol Pete, to tell everybody he meet.
   Tonight we need no rest, we gonna really throw a mess.
   We gonna knock down all the windows, we gonna kick down all the doors.
   We gonna pitch a wang dang doodle all night long.

3. Tell Fats and Washboard Sam that everybody gonna jam.
   Tell Shakin' Boxcar Joe, we got sawdust on the floor.
   Tell Peg and Caroline Dine, we gonna have a heck of a time.
   And when the fish scent fill the air, there'll be snuff juice everywhere.
   We gonna pitch a wang dang doodle all night long.

You Shook Me

Words and Music by Willie Dixon and J.B. Lenoir

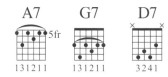

Key of D

Intro

Slow

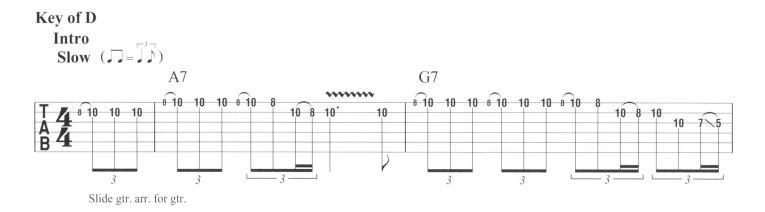

Slide gtr. arr. for gtr.

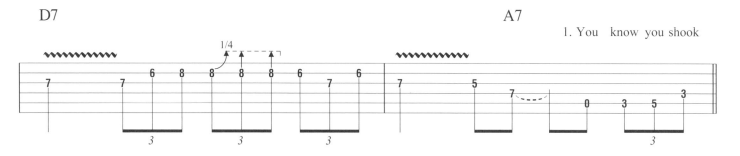

1. You know you shook

%. Verse

(4.) me, ba - by.   You shook me all   night long.

2., 3. *See additional lyrics*

You know you shook me, ba - by.

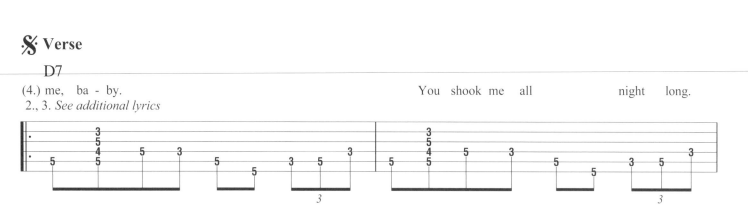

D7

You shook me all   night long.

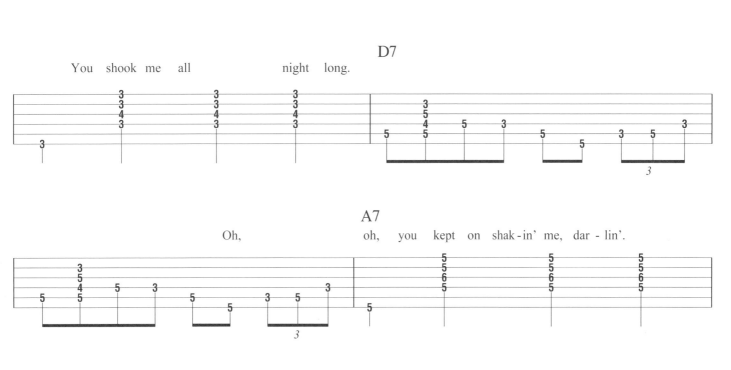

A7

Oh,   oh, you kept on shak-in' me, dar-lin'.

G7   D7

Oh,   oh, you messed up my hap-py home.

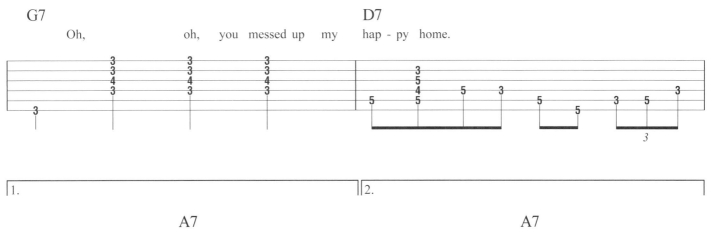

1.   2.

A7   A7

2. You know you moves   3. Oh,

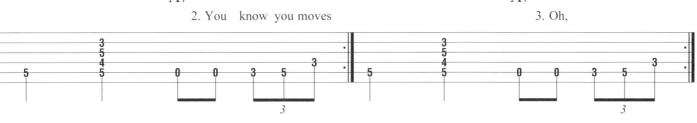

3.

D.S. and fade

A7

4. You know you shook

Additional Lyrics

2. You know you moves me, baby, just like a hurricane.
   You know you moves me, baby, just like a hurricane.
   Oh, you know you move me, darlin', just like an earthquake move the land.

3. Oh, sometime I wonder what my poor wife and child gonna do.
   Oh, sometime I wonder what my poor wife and child gonna do.
   Oh, you know that you made me mistreat them, darling. Whoa, I'm madly in love with you.

RHYTHM TAB LEGEND

Rhythm Tab is a form of notation that adds rhythmic values to the traditional tab staff.

TABLATURE graphically represents the guitar fingerboard. Each horizontal line represents a string, and each number represents a fret. Rhythmic values are shown using ovals, stems, and dots.

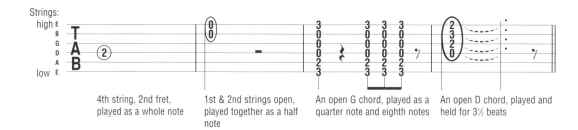

4th string, 2nd fret, played as a whole note

1st & 2nd strings open, played together as a half note

An open G chord, played as a quarter note and eighth notes

An open D chord, played and held for 3½ beats

Definitions for Special Guitar Notation

HALF-STEP BEND: Strike the note and bend up 1/2 step.

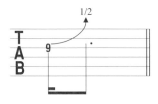

WHOLE-STEP BEND: Strike the note and bend up one step.

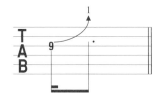

SLIGHT (MICROTONE) BEND: Strike the note and bend up 1/4 step.

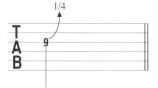

BEND AND RELEASE: Strike the note and bend up as indicated, then release back to the original note. Only the first note is struck.

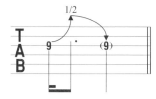

PRE-BEND: Bend the note as indicated, then strike it.

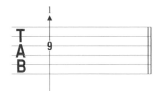

GRACE NOTE PRE-BEND AND RELEASE: Bend the note as indicated. Strike it and release the bend back to the original note.

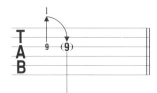

UNISON BEND: Strike the two notes simultaneously and bend the lower note up to the pitch of the higher.

HOLD BEND: While sustaining bent note, strike note on different string.

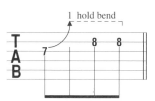

VIBRATO: The string is vibrated by rapidly bending and releasing the note with the fretting hand.

WIDE VIBRATO: The pitch is varied to a greater degree by vibrating with the fretting hand.

HAMMER-ON: Strike the first (lower) note with one finger, then sound the higher note (on the same string) with another finger by fretting it without picking.

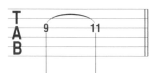

PULL-OFF: Place both fingers on the notes to be sounded. Strike the first note and without picking, pull the finger off to sound the second (lower) note.

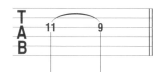

HAMMER FROM NOWHERE: Sound note(s) by hammering with fret hand finger only.

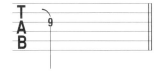

GRACE NOTE SLUR: Strike the note and immediately hammer-on (or pull-off) as indicated.

GRACE NOTE SLUR (CLUSTER): Strike the notes and immediately hammer-on (or pull-off) as indicated.

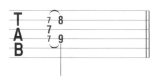

LEGATO SLIDE: Strike the first note and then slide the same fret-hand finger up or down to the second note. The second note is not struck.

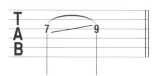

SHIFT SLIDE: Same as legato slide, except the second note is struck.

GRACE NOTE SLIDE: Quickly slide into the note from below or above.

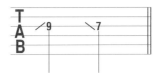

TRILL: Very rapidly alternate between the notes indicated by continuously hammering on and pulling off.

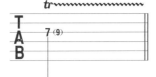

TAPPING: Hammer ("tap") the fret indicated with the pick-hand index or middle finger and pull off to the note fretted by the fret hand.

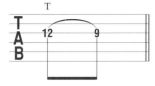

NATURAL HARMONIC: Strike the note while the fret-hand lightly touches the string directly over the fret indicated.

Harm.

PINCH HARMONIC: The note is fretted normally and a harmonic is produced by adding the edge of the thumb or the tip of the index finger of the pick hand to the normal pick attack.

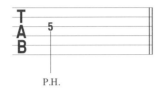

P.H.

HARP HARMONIC: The note is fretted normally and a harmonic is produced by gently resting the pick hand's index finger directly above the indicated fret (in parentheses) while the pick hand's thumb or pick assists by plucking the appropriate string.

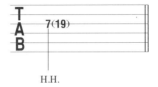

H.H.

PICK SCRAPE: The edge of the pick is rubbed down (or up) the string, producing a scratchy sound.

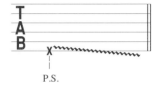

P.S.

MUFFLED STRINGS: A percussive sound is produced by laying the fret hand across the string(s) without depressing, and striking them with the pick hand.

PALM MUTING: The note is partially muted by the pick hand lightly touching the string(s) just before the bridge.

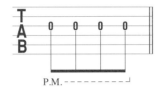

P.M. - - - - - - - - - ⌐

RAKE: Drag the pick across the strings indicated with a single motion.

rake - ⌐

TREMOLO PICKING: The note is picked as rapidly and continuously as possible.

ARPEGGIATE: Play the notes of the chord indicated by quickly rolling them from bottom to top.

VIBRATO BAR DIVE AND RETURN: The pitch of the note or chord is dropped a specified number of steps (in rhythm), then returned to the original pitch.

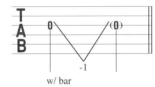

w/ bar

VIBRATO BAR SCOOP: Depress the bar just before striking the note, then quickly release the bar.

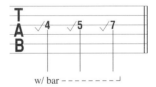

w/ bar - - - - - - - - ⌐

VIBRATO BAR DIP: Strike the note and then immediately drop a specified number of steps, then release back to the original pitch.

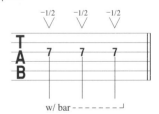

w/ bar - - - - - - ⌐

Additional Musical Definitions

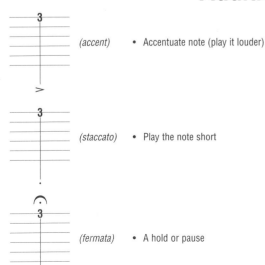

(accent) • Accentuate note (play it louder)

(staccato) • Play the note short

(fermata) • A hold or pause

⊓ • Downstroke

∨ • Upstroke

• Repeat measures between signs

NOTE: Tablature numbers in parentheses are used when:
• The note is sustained, but a new articulation begins (such as a hammer-on, pull-off, slide, or bend), or
• A bend is released.
• A note sustains while crossing from one staff to another.

FIRST 50

Books in the First 50 series contain easy to intermediate arrangements for must-know songs. Each arrangement is simple and streamlined, yet still captures the essence of the tune.

First 50 Baroque Pieces
You Should Play on Guitar
Includes selections by Johann Sebastian Bach, Robert de Visée, Ernst Gottlieb Baron, Santiago de Murcia, Antonio Vivaldi, Sylvius Leopold Weiss, and more.
00322567..................................$14.99

First 50 Bluegrass Solos
You Should Play on Guitar
I Am a Man of Constant Sorrow • Long Journey Home • Molly and Tenbrooks • Old Joe Clark • Rocky Top • Salty Dog Blues • and more.
00298574..................................$15.99

First 50 Blues Songs
You Should Play on Guitar
All Your Love (I Miss Loving) • Bad to the Bone • Born Under a Bad Sign • Dust My Broom • Hoodoo Man Blues • Little Red Rooster • Love Struck Baby • Pride and Joy • Smoking Gun • Still Got the Blues • The Thrill Is Gone • You Shook Me • and more.
00235790..................................$17.99

First 50 Blues Turnarounds
You Should Play on Guitar
You'll learn cool turnarounds in the styles of these jazz legends: John Lee Hooker, Robert Johnson, Joe Pass, Jimmy Rogers, Hubert Sumlin, Stevie Ray Vaughan, T-Bone Walker, Muddy Waters, and more.
00277469..................................$14.99

First 50 Chords
You Should Play on Guitar
American Pie • Back in Black • Brown Eyed Girl • Landslide • Let It Be • Riptide • Summer of '69 • Take Me Home, Country Roads • Won't Get Fooled Again • You've Got a Friend • and more.
00300255 Guitar..................................$12.99

First 50 Classical Pieces
You Should Play on Guitar
Includes compositions by J.S. Bach, Augustin Barrios, Matteo Carcassi, Domenico Scarlatti, Fernando Sor, Francisco Tárrega, Robert de Visée, Antonio Vivaldi and many more.
00155414 ....$15.99

First 50 Folk Songs
You Should Play on Guitar
Amazing Grace • Down by the Riverside • Home on the Range • I've Been Working on the Railroad • Kumbaya • Man of Constant Sorrow • Oh! Susanna • This Little Light of Mine • When the Saints Go Marching In • The Yellow Rose of Texas • and more.
00235868 ....$15.99

First 50 Guitar Duets
You Should Play
Chopsticks • Clocks • Eleanor Rigby • Game of Thrones Theme • Hallelujah • Linus and Lucy (from *A Charlie Brown Christmas*) • Memory (from *Cats*) • Over the Rainbow (from *The Wizard of Oz*) • Star Wars (Main Theme) • What a Wonderful World • You Raise Me Up • and more.
00319706..................................$14.99

First 50 Jazz Standards
You Should Play on Guitar
All the Things You Are • Body and Soul • Don't Get Around Much Anymore • Fly Me to the Moon (In Other Words) • The Girl from Ipanema (Garota De Ipanema) • I Got Rhythm • Laura • Misty • Night and Day • Satin Summertime • When I Fall in Love • and more.
00198594 Solo Guitar..................................$15.99

First 50 Kids' Songs
You Should Play on Guitar
Do-Re-Mi • Hakuna Matata • Let It Go • My Favorite Things • Puff the Magic Dragon • Take Me Out to the Ball Game • Won't You Be My Neighbor? (It's a Beautiful Day in the Neighborhood) • and more.
00300500 ....$15.99

First 50 Licks
You Should Play on Guitar
Licks presented include the styles of legendary guitarists like Eric Clapton, Buddy Guy, Jimi Hendrix, B.B. King, Randy Rhoads, Carlos Santana, Stevie Ray Vaughan and many more.
00278875 Book/Online Audio..................................$14.99

First 50 Riffs
You Should Play on Guitar
All Right Now • Back in Black • Barracuda • Carry on Wayward Son • Crazy Train • La Grange • Layla • Seven Nation Army • Smoke on the Water • Sunday Bloody Sunday • Sunshine of Your Love • Sweet Home Alabama • Working Man • and more.
00277366..................................$12.99

First 50 Rock Songs You Should
Play on Electric Guitar
All Along the Watchtower • Beat It • Brown Eyed Girl • Cocaine • Detroit Rock City • Hallelujah • (I Can't Get No) Satisfaction • Oh, Pretty Woman • Pride and Joy • Seven Nation Army • Should I Stay or Should I Go • Smells like Teen Spirit • Smoke on the Water • When I Come Around • You Really Got Me • and more.
00131159..................................$15.99

First 50 Songs by the Beatles You
Should Play on Guitar
All You Need Is Love • Blackbird • Come Together • Eleanor Rigby • Hey Jude • I Want to Hold Your Hand • Let It Be • Ob-La-Di, Ob-La-Da • She Loves You • Twist and Shout • Yellow Submarine • Yesterday • and more.
00295323..................................$19.99

First 50 Songs
You Should Fingerpick on Guitar
Annie's Song • Blackbird • The Boxer • Classical Gas • Dust in the Wind • Fire and Rain • Greensleeves • Road Trippin' • Shape of My Heart • Tears in Heaven • Time in a Bottle • Vincent (Starry Starry Night) • and more.
00149269..................................$15.99

First 50 Songs You Should
Play on 12-String Guitar
California Dreamin' • Closer to the Heart • Free Fallin' • Give a Little Bit • Hotel California • Leaving on a Jet Plane • Life by the Drop • Over the Hills and Far Away • Solsbury Hill • Space Oddity • Wish You Were Here • You Wear It Well • and more.
00287559..................................$15.99

First 50 Songs You Should Play on
Acoustic Guitar
Against the Wind • Boulevard of Broken Dreams • Champagne Supernova • Every Rose Has Its Thorn • Fast Car • Free Fallin' • Layla • Let Her Go • Mean • One • Ring of Fire • Signs • Stairway to Heaven • Trouble • Wagon Wheel • Yellow • Yesterday • and more.
00131209..................................$15.99

First 50 Songs
You Should Play on Bass
Blister in the Sun • I Got You (I Feel Good) • Livin' on a Prayer • Low Rider • Money • Monkey Wrench • My Generation • Roxanne • Should I Stay or Should I Go • Uptown Funk • What's Going On • With or Without You • Yellow • and more.
00149189..................................$15.99

First 50 Songs
You Should Play on Solo Guitar
Africa • All of Me • Blue Skies • California Dreamin' • Change the World • Crazy • Dream a Little Dream of Me • Every Breath You Take • Hallelujah • Wonderful Tonight • Yesterday • You Raise Me Up • Your Song • and more.
00288843..................................$16.99

First 50 Songs
You Should Strum on Guitar
American Pie • Blowin' in the Wind • Daughter • Hey, Soul Sister • Home • I Will Wait • Losing My Religion • Mrs. Robinson • No Woman No Cry • Peaceful Easy Feeling • Rocky Mountain High • Sweet Caroline • Teardrops on My Guitar • Wonderful Tonight • and more.
00148996 Guitar..................................$15.99

HAL•LEONARD®
www.halleonard.com

0421
014

Prices, contents and availability subject to change without notice.